SACRED TIME
unRemembered

Tracing Christian~~~
Foremost F~~~

By definition, an *enigma* is a puzzling or mystifying person, thing or situation. At the creation of the world, the Creator specified "sacred time" to be remembered (Exodus 20:8). Yet, for centuries, the original "Lord's day" God specified has been forgotten.

How was this divine institution from the Creation summarily abandoned, and who is responsible? This is Christianity's foremost enigma, and this book tells its amazing story.

By Daniel Knauft with Kevin Morgan

It had been a tiring ten-hour trip traveling south by train from Berlin. Now we had arrived at our highly anticipated destination—history-rich Rome—the "eternal city." During the next few days, my three history buff companions and I would tour the landmarks of the Coliseum, the Roman Forum, the Castle of St. Angelo and the Vatican sites, including St. Peter's Basilica. I would make numerous vital discoveries in this ancient city dating from the seventh century before Christ.

After parking my luggage in our hotel suite, my tired eyes were drawn to an Italian calendar on the wall. It was the first time I had seen a calendar outside America. Tomorrow would be Saturday, and on the wall calendar, surprisingly, the word for Saturday in Italian riveted me—*Sabato*. I already knew that people who speak Spanish, Russian, Polish, Arabic, Portuguese, Czech, Serbian, Croatian, and Hebrew use this word *"Sabbath"* to identify the seventh day of the week.* But was the seventh day also "Sabbath" in Italy, the home of the Roman Catholic Church, where Sunday is the honored day?

I stared to make sure I was reading it correctly. There was no mistaking it—in Italian, the word designating the seventh day of the week is *Sabato*—"Sabbath." This is the very day of the week the Bible says the Creator of our world originally "blessed" and set apart as holy time. It is the special day referred to in the fourth of the Ten Commandments (the third commandment in Catholic catechisms) in Exodus 20:8–11.

Here I was—in Rome. In a day or two we would visit the Roman Catholic churches of Saint John Lateran and the Church of Jesus Christ (the home church of Ignatius Loyola)—two of 300 Catholic cathedrals and churches in this historic city. Each of these churches is officially pastored by one of the many cardinals of the Catholic Church installed throughout the world.

A noticeable contrast flashed into my thinking. While my traveling companions and I would be attending a local Sabbath-observing Protestant church on *Sabato* just blocks from the Vatican, none of Rome's 300 Catholic churches—including St. Peter's basilica— would be open for weekly worship until Sunday, which the Catholic Church considers the "LORD's day." And so it has been for centuries.

---

* Remarkably, in 86 out of 160 ancient and modern languages, the name for the seventh day of the week is a form of the Hebrew *Shabbat*, meaning "rest."

A ripe and pertinent question

A question that curious churched and non-churched people often ask is: *How did the Christian church come to favor Sunday over the seventh-day Sabbath of Creation, of ancient Israel, and of Jesus Himself?*

This question has come down through the generations since medieval times, and it is as ripe for investigation and study today as it has always been. Many believe it is the most pressing of Christianity's unfinished business since the Protestant Reformation of the sixteenth century. *How could an honored weekly biblical institution rooted in Creation and practiced for thousands of years be replaced by another day without a word of mention from the Creator Himself? And what are the historical facts behind its replacement with the Sunday* LORD's *Day?*

COVER PHOTO: The dome of St. Peter's Basilica in Rome was designed by Michelangelo and later finished by Giacoma della Porta in 1590.

Your comments and questions for the author are welcome by email at:
deknauft@hotmail.com

Documentation verification and editing by Kevin L. Morgan
Copy editing by Wendy Marcum, David Jarnes, and Kevin L. Morgan
Cover design by Larson Creatives, Inc.
Book formatting by Aaron Troia
Cover photo by istock
Text type set in Bergamo 10/12 regular

Copyright © 2014 by Daniel Knauft
Published and distributed by:
Torchlight Intelligence Publishing
P. O. Box 135
Fall City, Washington 98024

Unless otherwise specified, Scripture references are from the New King James Version, Thomas Nelson Publisher's, © 1979, 1980, 1982, and are quoted in harmony with the publishers' stated policy.

About the Author

Author and publisher Daniel Knauft, M.Div., has thirty years of experience in pastoral ministry. He is a graduate of the Andrews University Theological Seminary in Berrien Springs, Michigan. For five years he was associate director of the Northwest Evangelism Institute in the Seattle, Washington area. In 2006 Knauft published the documentary-style book *Search for the Immortal Soul*. Other published titles are *Our Inhabited Universe*, *The Crucifixion Story*, *UFOs Unmasked*, *The Flood*, and *Mr. Ugly and Ten Other Short Stories*. Currently he is volunteer coordinator for All for Jesus Associates, a parachurch ministry leading Christian men and women to active personal witness suited to individual spiritual gifts.

Websites: torchlightintelligence.com   surgeinamerica.com

Table of Contents

Where were you when I laid the foundations of the earth?
—The Creator (Job 38:4)

CHAPTER 1
Creating Original Love

The weekly cycle is God's idea. In the Genesis Creation account, the *seventh day* is mentioned three times, while the previous six days are individually mentioned only once. Only one of the week's seven days was "blessed" and distinguished as being "hallowed"—it is the *seventh*. By "resting" on that first seventh day, the Creator inaugurated a weekly cycle of rest for the human family made in His image (Genesis 2:1–3).

Seminary professor Jiri Moskala noted that while the creation of human beings is the crowning act of the physical Creation, the *seventh day* is Creation week's climactic event because this day puts humans in relationship with their Maker. He wrote: "Sabbath is first of all about a relationship of beauty and splendor, of God with humans and humans with God."[1] Author Des Cummings, Jr., described the pathos of this day as "original love" and portrayed the Sabbath as "our personal Mount of Transfiguration—the place where we hear our heavenly Father say, 'This is My beloved child.' "[2] Dr. Norman Gulley, author and specialist on last-day events, called the Sabbath experience "God close up."[3]

Jesus reminds us: " '. . . the Sabbath was made for man' " (Mark 2:27)—for the whole human family. Two institutions originating prior to the entrance of sin survive to this day—marriage and the Sabbath day. They were designed at the Creation to maintain wholesome human happiness. These sister institutions, created within hours of each other, fulfill human relationships horizontally and vertically.

While the physical creation characterized the first six days, what was created on the *seventh day* is of a different nature—it was sacred *time*, a reality that cannot be tasted, touched, seen or heard. *Time* is the element in which we experience relationships. God designed the Sabbath day to enable humans to know Him intimately. He refers to it as His sign (Ezekiel 20:12, 20). Like a lover wooing the heart of his beloved, He passionately urges us to "remember"—remember the sacred, intimate, protected time He wants us to spend with Him (Exodus 20:8).

Christian author and former secularist Clifford Goldstein wrote:

Holy cities can be burned. . . . Holy shrines can be looted. But *time* is beyond the fire and the knife. No man can touch, much less destroy it. Therefore, by making a special time holy, God has made His Sabbath invincible, placing it in an element beyond the reach of any devices of mankind. Armies can sack cities. Rulers can ban pilgrimages. But no military tank—no swirl of ink—can keep away the seventh day. We can no more stop the Sabbath than the sunset. God protected His memorial to His created objects in space— which are vulnerable to man—by placing it in time, which is not. (*Heaven's Tender Touch,* Hart Research Center, Fallbrook, California, 1993)

The Creation event, as described in Genesis 1 and 2, is like a copyright or patent of the Creator. The Creator's signature is embedded in every cell and atom. God has no competitor as Creator of this planet of interrelated complexity of living forms. There is no alternative explanation that merits notice for the origin of the earth and its vast variety of exquisitely designed organisms and creatures. An orderly Creation is reality, and it is the springboard for understanding genuine science. Believers who weekly observe the seventh-day Sabbath of Creation testify to their noble, purposeful origin at the hand of their loving Creator, and they declare that the deeper meanings of life can only be found in an active relationship with Him—"God with humans and humans with God."

Brandeis University professor Nahum Sarna agrees: "Its observance is a declaration of faith . . . that the universe is wholly the purposeful product of divine intelligence, the work of a transcendent Being outside of nature and sovereign over space and time."[4] Professor Jiri Moskala noted: "By living Sabbath, believers are showing total devotion and respect to the holy Creator."[5] Australian writer Aleta Bainbridge wrote: "By worshiping on the seventh-day Sabbath, His people proclaim their allegiance to God as the rightful ruler of the universe, their Creator and Redeemer."[6]

To those who would cherish refuge in their Maker's weekly temple in time, God Himself has promised that they will " 'ride upon the high places of the earth' " (Isaiah 58:13, 14, KJV). To "ride high" with God—to revere and enjoy Him—is the greatest experience humans can have.

God has never withdrawn this promise. Has He transferred it to another day of the week—specifically to Sunday?

Why would such a transfer be necessary?

Christians have long answered this question by maintaining that they observe Sunday in honor of the resurrection of Christ. Truly, the Resurrection is the divine ratification of Jesus' victory over sin and a divine promise that all the universe ultimately will be secure from God's enemy. Christ's tomb is empty! He is risen! Let Him be glorified!

With all due kindness, we must ask every Christian believer, whether pastor, professor, priest, pope or Bible student: *Why would Christians need to abandon the sacred, seventh-day Sabbath of Creation and the fourth commandment, which magnifies the redeeming Creator God, in order to honor the resurrection of Jesus? Why should one cancel out the other? Do not Creation and Redemption walk hand in hand? Do they not both stand as the transcendent handiwork of our merciful and loving God?*

For millions of Christians throughout the centuries, Sunday has been the day on which to express devotion and worship to Jesus through preaching the gospel, Bible teaching and Christian fellowship. Through God-fearing ministries and worldwide missionary services on that day, untold thousands have found their way to Christ and His saving power.

Yet, during these same centuries, many earnest, Bible-believing scholars and honest-hearted devotees of Jesus have recognized that there is a major biblical disconnect in the institution of Sunday as the "LORD's day." Note these three brief points of Bible reasoning:

First, Jesus Himself designated the particular day of His choosing by declaring that He, the Son of Man, bears this divine title—" 'LORD of the Sabbath' " (Mark 2:28).*

Second, the fourth commandment, which is part of the universal and perpetual law of God, has already designated the seventh-day of the weekly cycle as the LORD's *day* (Exodus 20:8–11; Isaiah 58:13). As such, it bears the credentials of the Most High God.

Third, immediately following his conversion, Paul, the apostle to the Gentiles, was led to Arabia and then to Damascus for a period of three years, during which time he was taught by the LORD through "the revelation of Jesus Christ" (Galatians 1:11–20). Throughout Paul's New Testament writings, which are drawn from his personal instruction from Jesus, there is not a single line of thought tying weekly recognition of the resurrection of Jesus to the first day of the week. Rather, Paul directly connects the death, burial and resurrection of Christ—which is the heart of the New Testament gospel message—with baptism (Romans 6:3–6). Upon being "filled with the Holy Spirit," Paul immediately affirmed Christ's death and resurrection through water baptism (Acts 9:17, 18). And, interestingly, Paul himself provides the most prominent example of on-going Sabbath observance among Jewish and Gentile believers in the early church (see Acts 13:42–44; 16:13; 17:2; 18:4).

With this in view, the question of the authority by which Sunday has been designated the "LORD's day" is significant.

Who has authority over divine institutions?

The question of authority is well established in Scripture. Every human who has ever lived on this planet is indebted to the LORD Jesus Christ for having bought us with His shed blood and bearing the sins of the whole world upon Himself at the cross (1 Corinthians 6:20). As Sovereign LORD, He is the "Chief Cornerstone"

---

* Unless otherwise specified, all Bible references are from the New King James Version (NKJV),©1979,1980,1982edition,ThomasNelsonPublishers,Inc.,Nashville,Tennessee.

(Ephesians 2:20; 1 Peter 2:6). All human leadership, whether domestic, intellectual, political or ecclesiastical, is obligated to act in submission to His lordship.

One of the last things Jesus said before returning to the courts of heaven was: "All authority has been given to Me in heaven and on earth" (Matthew 28:18). In modern parlance, this means that the risen Christ is the CEO of all the universe and, in particular, of this planet. His credentials no one can rival.

In speaking to the religious leaders, Jesus earlier referred to Himself in metaphor as the "Shepherd" of the sheep and as the "Door" of the sheepfold. He declared that all who attempt to gain access to the sheepfold some other way are impostors—they are thieves, robbers, hirelings or strangers (John 10:1–18).

Only one Person has been authorized to officially represent and carry forward Jesus' mission of providing salvation on earth—the Holy Spirit, the divine equal of Jesus. Even still, He leads within the parameters that Jesus set forth: " '. . . when He, the Spirit of truth, has come, He will guide you into all truth; for He will not speak on His own authority, . . . He will glorify Me, for He will take of what is Mine and declare it to you' " (John 16:13, 14).

This leads us to ask: *Has Jesus—"the Good Shepherd"—authorized in Scripture the dismantling of the "blessed" and "hallowed" seventh-day Sabbath and the instituting of Sunday in its place, or is this change the cunning deed of a "hireling or a stranger," in the words of Jesus?*

We must answer this question according to Christianity's only true authority. Jesus identified what this is in the simple but profound words: " 'I am the good shepherd. . . . My sheep hear My voice, and I know them, and they follow Me. . . . Yet they will by no means follow a stranger, but will flee from him, for they do not know the voice of strangers' " (John 10:11, 27, 5).

How should it be decided?

Many who have been led to investigate this matter are moved by an honest desire to know the facts of the Bible and church history. I recognize that most people reading these words have long-standing religious traditions and deep-seated emotions tied to their observance of Sunday. However, serious Bible students, in their search for the truth, must courageously discard the religious pluralism and relativism of our modern culture.

Individually, we must each decide how we will determine issues of faith and belief. Will it be by what feels right, by a hunch, or by cultural leanings? And are we merely to pass on to the next generation centuries old cherished traditions? One contemporary Christian radio commentator wisely counseled: "We should be asking: Is this true or is this just what you were taught?"[7]

Is the Bible not still Christianity's highest authority and only authoritative source of absolute truth and the expressed will of God? Biblical scholar Clinton Wahlen offered this reason for the unique status of Scripture:

[The Bible] stands above and independent of organized ecclesiastical authorities because it is a revelation of God Himself. In obeying its precepts we obey the God who is the author and revealer of those principles, and grant to His words and to His person the respect their transcendent authority deserves.[8]

With this in view, will we then allow Scripture to have the "right to impose obligation on the human conscience," as theologian R. C. Sproul has put it?[9] Will the revealed will of God override mere human inclination, speculation and invention?

Referring to the struggle between the subjective and objective in deciding issues of faith, highly respected British theologian and author, the late John R. W. Stott advised: "Our emotions are a fluctuating, unreliable guide to truth and must not be exalted to the place of supreme authority in determining it. As a committed Evangelical, my question must be—and is—not what my heart tells me, but what does God's word say?"[10]

I did not cease to warn everyone night and day with tears.
—*The* Apostle Paul (Acts 20:31)

CHAPTER 2
On Stage: The Testimony of History

Centuries have passed since the unfolding of events described in this chapter. Most people today have only a vague knowledge of what happened during the early centuries following the earthly ministry of Jesus Christ. Three focal points in church history provide a context for this unfolding drama: doctrinal division, weekly worship practice, and the role of the Day of Pentecost. We will take these in their order.

1. Doctrinal division. During the first five hundred years of Christianity, conflict over doctrinal beliefs and Christian practice began to divide Christians theologically as well as geographically into two main groups.

In 2 Thessalonians, Paul, the apostle to the Gentiles, forecast a major departure from Christian belief and warned that the process of change had already begun in his day (2 Thessalonians 2:3–7). He expected some leaders of the church to disregard the original, apostolic Christian faith and make major alterations in Christian doctrine and practice (Acts 20:29, 30).

What Paul had warned about soon took place. In the early centuries, **Western Christianity,** which was centered in Rome, began to develop a style of ecclesiastical leadership in which church and political entities were combined. In its attempts to make converts, the church gradually adapted its message and practices to the prevailing culture. It began to bring under the umbrella of Christian thought beliefs that were contrary to Christianity's original teachings.

In the religions of the non-Christian population, the first day of the week was already favored as a day dedicated to the sun. Roman Christianity's primary theological mutation, born out of an urgency to distinguish herself from Jewish practice, was the adoption of Sunday, the day on which pagans honored their supreme deity, as the "LORD's day" in place of the seventh-day Sabbath. Scholar Samuele Bacchiocchi described this:

The role that the Church of Rome played in causing the abandonment of the Sabbath and the adoption of Sunday has been underestimated, if not totally neglected, in recent studies. . . . It is there that we found both the circumstances and the authority necessary to accomplish such a liturgical change. . . . (*From Sabbath to Sunday*, The Pontifical Gregorian University Press, Rome, 1977, p. 211)

Secular historians, as well, describe a major shift early in the fourth century in the worship practice of Christians under Rome's influence:

Under his [Constantine's] regime Sunday became the Christian Sabbath. . . . (Jay Tolson and Linda Kulman, "The Real Jesus," *U.S. News and World Report,* March 8, 2004, p. 44)

So, what was the line of thought of Christian leaders at the heart of the Empire at this time? A spokesman for the Church of Rome has explained the rationale behind this human alteration in Christian practice:

The church took the pagan philosophy and made it the buckler of faith against the heathen. . . . She took the pagan Sunday and made it the Christian Sunday. . . . There is, in truth, something royal, kingly about the sun, making it a fit emblem of Jesus, the Sun of Justice. Hence the church in these countries would seem to have said, "Keep that old, pagan name. It shall remain consecrated, sanctified." And thus, the pagan Sunday, dedicated to Balder, became the

Christian Sunday, sacred to Jesus. (William L. Gildea, *The Catholic World*, March 1894, p. 809)

Justin Martyr's apology to Roman Emperor Antoninus Pius in the second century provides one of the earliest hints that the church at Rome had transferred to a Sunday assembly. His case to the emperor was skillfully built by the connecting of light and the sun with the resurrection of Jesus, a point of reasoning that a pagan Roman emperor would appreciate and an explanation that would quiet misunderstood opposition to a "Jewish" institution—the seventh-day Sabbath, from which Christians at Rome, including Justin Martyr, were distancing themselves:

> . . . **Sunday is the day on which we all hold our common assembly because it is the first day on which God, having wrought a change in the darkness in matter, made the world: and Jesus Christ our Saviour on the same day rose from the dead. For He was crucified on the day before that of Saturn [Saturday]; and on the day after that of Saturn, which is the day of the Sun, having appeared to His apostles and disciples** . . . (Apology to Emperor Antoninus Pius, chap. 67, in *Ante-Nicene Fathers*, vol. 1, pp. 185, 186)

With the popularization of Christianity under Emperor Constantine's reign, there was a resulting mingling of pagan ritual and practice with the Church of Rome. The consequences of a departure from primitive Christianity became apparent even to non-Christian citizens in Rome. Highly reputed teacher, preacher and debater bishop Faustus of Milevis employed the following observation in accusing St. Augustine:

> **You celebrate the solemn festivals of the Gentiles, their calends, and their solstices; and as to their manners, those you have retained without any alteration. Nothing distinguishes you from the pagans except that you hold your assemblies apart from them.** (Quoted by John Jortin, *Discourses*

Concerning the Truth of the Christian Religion, Richard Taylor and Company, London, 1805, vol. 2, p. 123)

In time, the Western church of medieval times became the paramount religious force in Europe with the Pope of Rome as its overseer and religious-political leader. A major feature of this wing of Christianity was its sweeping world-view that the Church is the mediatorial advocate between God and humans. This resulted in a separation of roles between clergy and laity, a priesthood, monasteries and a system of canon law. Jerome's Latin Vulgate translation, which the common people could not understand, became the official Bible and remained so for centuries. Interpretation of this sacred Book was relegated to the ecclesiastical leadership.

Eastern Christianity, the other branch of Christian thought and practice, was centered first in Jerusalem and later in Syrian Antioch. It followed more closely the missionary style and teaching of the first century church of the disciples and apostles. Its teachers and evangelists carried its simple teachings of the Scriptures from outpost training centers across continents—from Ireland and England to Asia Minor, Persia, India and other parts of Asia. Its core teaching that each believer is responsible before God led to personal dedication and discipleship under the gifts of the Holy Spirit. Its scholars and bishops became defenders of the original Christian faith of the disciples and apostles, and they became staunch opponents of the perversion of the Old and New Testament texts.

A distinguishing feature of Eastern Christianity, which highlighted its differences with Western Christianity, was its continued observance of the seventh-day Sabbath—even when they were also observing Sunday:

> **As for the Saturday, that retained wonted credit in the Eastern Church, little inferior to the LORD's day, if not plainly equal: . . . S[aint] *Athanasius* Patriarch there, affirms that they assembled on the *Sabbath days,* not that they were infected any whit with Judaisms which was far from them, but that they came together on the Sabbath day, to worship Jesus the LORD of the Sabbath. . . . it seems that Saturday was held**

in a far esteem, and joined together with the Sunday. . . . (Dr. Peter Heylyn, *History of the Sabbath,* Henry Seile, London, 1636, Part II, Chapter 3, par. 5, pp. 73–75, spelling modernized)

The disciple Thomas brought Christianity and the observance of the seventh-day Sabbath to India in the first century. Up until the eleventh century, this wing of Christianity practiced the seventh-day Sabbath even though the Western church of medieval times had declared this practice heretical. Persecution and harassment eventually forced the Eastern church underground. Preserved through troublesome times, many of its teachings once again became prominent in the Protestant Reformation. This wing of Christianity is sometimes identified as the church in "the wilderness" (Revelation 12:14).

Unfortunately, most people today are not aware of the significant role that this branch of Christianity played, and we are left to ponder: *What is the fundamental difference between these two streams of Christianity?*

Professional educator and researcher Edwin de Kock provided the following summary: "Christianity . . . split into two main groups: those who closely adhered to the Scriptures, as Jesus and the apostles had done, and those who mixed their religion with elements that neither the Old nor the New Testament sanctioned. Much like the Scribes and Pharisees in the time of our LORD, the latter departed from the *sola scriptura* principle [the Bible only], adding many human traditions, some taken over from Paganism. These believers were the majority and became the dominant strain of Christianity, inclined to persecute those who would not follow them into apostasy."[11]

2. Weekly worship practice. A widespread belief among Christians worldwide today is that Sunday observance has always been universal among Christians ever since the resurrection of Jesus and the launching of the Christian church on the Day of Pentecost. This is a major misconception.

There is no pattern of first day assembly in the New Testament. That Jesus was resurrected on the first day of the week is a certainty, but documentation for when the first Christians gathered for assembly and worship leads in another direction. So where does the evidence in the New Testament take us?

16

Interestingly, the biblical evidence for a pattern of weekly gatherings of Jewish and Gentile Christians is found outside the first established center of the Christian faith in Jerusalem and Judea. Logically, the pattern set by the mother church would be the one brought to the missionary territories as believers in Jesus expanded their evangelistic efforts beyond Judea and Galilee (Acts 1:8). It is in these new regions that we find definite answers.

Nearly thirty years after the crucifixion, Luke, physician and Gentile author of the Acts of the Apostles, described how the Apostle Paul and his missionary team, following the first Jerusalem council, worshiped with first century Gentile believers at the city of Philippi. This is Luke's eyewitness account:

And on the Sabbath day we went out of the city to the riverside, where prayer was customarily made; and we sat down and spoke to the women who met there. (Acts 16:13)

Again, it is Paul's experiences that build the case for the day upon which weekly assembly of Jewish and Gentile believers occurred. As an apostle, Paul had the credentials of being "sent" by the brethren of the Jerusalem Council. He was an eyewitness that Jesus was risen from the grave, having been under the tutelage of the "revelation of Jesus Christ" (Galatians 1:12).

Luke has recorded exceptional interest in Paul's preaching in the city of Antioch of Asia Minor, ranked by Josephus as the third largest city in the Roman Empire: "And when the Jews went out of the synagogue, the Gentiles begged that these words might be preached to them the next Sabbath. . . . And the next Sabbath almost the whole city came together to hear the word of God" (Acts 13:42–44).

Some argue that Paul's strategy for reaching new territories was to adopt the customary meeting times of the local people. For Jews, this would be the Sabbath. But if a new day, the first day of the week, was to be the new Christian custom for weekly assembly, there is no record that Paul ever taught or mentioned it in any of his writings. Rather, Paul consistently connected a memorial for the resurrection of Jesus with believer's baptism (Romans 6:3–5; Colossians 2:12).

On his second evangelistic tour, Paul spent considerable time building up the Corinthian church. It was enough time to demonstrate his chosen pattern of weekly ministry and preaching, as recorded by Luke: "And he reasoned in the synagogue every Sabbath, and persuaded both Jews and Greeks. . . . And he continued there a year and six months, teaching the word of God among them" (Acts 18:4, 11).

If Paul and the Corinthian Christians observed a first day assembly in honor of the LORD's resurrection, Paul never wrote of it, and Paul's personal physician, Luke, placed no significance on it in his record in the book of the Acts of the Apostles. Paul's chosen pattern of ministry, on display in Corinth, is classic New Testament and New Covenant practice. Paul is the author of the book of Galatians, which affirmed that believers are the "Israel of God" (Galatians 6:16), and many believe him to be the writer of the epistle to the Hebrews, in which he upheld Sabbath observance for believers. (See Supporting Exhibit #5, on page 163.) He has affirmed the ministry pattern set by Jesus Christ (Luke 4:16), Author and Cornerstone of the New Covenant (Matthew 26:26–29).

From the New Testament evidence, it is right to conclude that both the mother church and the multiplying churches in the missionary territories were observing the seventh day of the fourth commandment. Other church historians testify to this as well.

Curiously, the only mentions of the first day of the week in the New Testament are in Acts 20:7 and 1 Corinthians 16:2. The first instance was when Paul held a special Saturday evening meeting with the believers in Troas because he would be traveling the next day. The second was Paul's instruction to the members of the church in Corinth to set aside money at their home the first of every week to avoid fund-raising when he arrived.

Sabbath practice continues

Polycarp of Smyrna (A.D. 69–155) is a well-known figure of the second century. He was the younger contemporary of the disciple John, who was the pastor of the nearby church of Ephesus and Polycarp's mentor. It is believed that Polycarp repeated in his sermons many of the stories about Jesus Christ that he had heard from John.

Was Polycarp a Sabbath-observer? Existing records suggest that he was. Evidence from *The Life of Polycarp* says that John's disciple Polycarp was ordained a bishop in the church of Smyrna on the Sabbath (*The Life of Polycarp,* 22:1) and that he then met with the church for exhortation and Bible study the following Sabbath (*The Life of Polycarp,* 24:1). Polycarp was ultimately martyred as a Christian for refusing to acknowledge the emperor as god. His martyrdom purposely took place on the Sabbath, as a horrified crowd looked on (*Martyrdom of Polycarp,* 21:1).

Sabbath observance continued for centuries. Four hundred years after the resurrection of Christ, two separate church historians from the fifth century describe this widespread weekly Christian worship practice:

For although almost all churches throughout the world celebrate the sacred mysteries [the LORD's Supper] on the Sabbath of every week, yet the Christians of Alexandria and Rome, on account of some ancient tradition, have ceased to do this. (Socrates Scholasticus [c. A.D. 439], *Ecclesiastical History*, bk. 5, chap. 22, p. 289, in *Nicene and Post-Nicene Fathers,* second edition, vol. 2, p. 132)

The people of Constantinople, and almost everywhere, assemble together on the Sabbath, as well as on the first day of the week; which custom is never observed at Rome or at Alexandria. There are several cities and villages in Egypt where, contrary to the usage established elsewhere, the people meet together on Sabbath evenings, and, although they have dined previously, partake of the mysteries. (Hermias Sozomen [c. A.D. 460], *Ecclesiastical History*, bk. 7, chap. 19, in *Nicene and Post-Nicene Fathers,* second edition, vol. 2, p. 390)

That Gentile believers in the Roman Empire observed the seventh day is attested to by Dr. Paula Fredriksen, a historian of early Christianity and former chair of the Department of Religion at Boston University:

Fourth-century Gentile Christians, despite the anti-Jewish ideology of their own bishops, kept Saturday as their day of rest. . . . (Quoted by Jay Tolson and Linda Kulman, "The Real Jesus," *U.S. News and World Report*, March 8, 2004, p. 43)

Dr. Fredriksen's sweeping generalization in a national news magazine about Saturday's sacredness to Gentile Christians in the fourth century may come as a surprise to many in the twenty-first century. Yet, collective historical documentation overwhelmingly supports her statement. One such confirmation is that of Joseph Bingham (1668–1723) recorded in his exhaustive *Antiquities of the Christian Church* (and citing sources that we will see later in this book):

Next to the LORD's-Day the ancient Christians were very careful in the observation of Saturday, or the seventh day, which was the ancient Jewish sabbath. Some observed it as a fast, others as a festival; but all unanimously agreed in keeping it as a more solemn day of religious worship and adoration. In the Eastern church it was ever observed as a festival, one only sabbath exempted, which was called the Great Sabbath [and kept as a fast], between Good Friday and Easter-day. . . . From hence it is plain, that all the Oriental churches, and the greatest part of the world, observed the sabbath as a festival. . . . Athanasius [A.D. 296–373] likewise tells us, that they held religious assemblies on the sabbath, not because they were infected with Judaism, but to worship Jesus, the LORD of the sabbath. Epiphanius [A.D. 315–403] says the same, that it was a day of public assembly in many churches, meaning Oriental churches, where it was kept a festival." (*Antiquities of the Christian Church*, London, 1852, vol. II, bk. XX, chap. 3, sec. 1, pp. 1137, 1138)

In many areas of Western Europe early missionaries from Antioch and Asia Minor had planted the seeds of the apostolic faith, which included the observance of the Creation Sabbath. In northern Italy, the city of Milan would for many centuries be an outpost of evangelical fervor and a connecting link for Celtic Christianity in the West and Syrian Christianity in the East.

From Milan would come the first protests, beginning with Helvidius I (A.D. 300–360), against the theological irregularities coming into the church at Rome. (His writings defending the Christian faith were eventually destroyed.) Controversy erupted in the church at large over Rome's insistence that Saturday be observed as a fast.

Late in the fourth century, Ambrose, the celebrated Bishop of Milan (A.D. 374–397), said that, when he was in his home region, he observed Saturday. However, he also said that on his travels to Rome, he fasted on Saturday, as required, and he observed Sunday. Ambrose's statement, *Cum hies sum, non jejuno Sabbato; cum Rome sum jejuno Sabbato* [When I am here, I do not fast Saturday; when I was in Rome, I fasted on Saturday], gave rise to the proverb: "When in Rome, do as the Romans do." Augustine, the noted Bishop of Hippo in North Africa and contemporary of Ambrose, bemoaned the reality that, in two neighboring churches, one observed the seventh-day Sabbath, while the other fasted on it.[12]

Professor of Church History at Princeton University James C. Moffatt recorded the worship practice of early Christianity in the British Isles:

> **It seems to have been customary in the Celtic churches of early times, in Ireland as well as Scotland, to keep Saturday, the Jewish Sabbath, as a day of rest from labor, and Sunday, commemorative of the LORD's resurrection, as one of rejoicing, with exercises of public worship. . . . In that case they obeyed the fourth commandment literally upon the seventh day of the week—the day on which the LORD lay in the grave—and did not understand the precept about resting from labor to apply to the day of rejoicing over his resurrection. . . .** (*The Church in Scotland,* Presbyterian Board of Publication, Philadelphia, 1882, p. 140)

Evidence regarding Patrick, the renowned apostle to Ireland during the fifth century who never quoted the church fathers or referenced the canons of church councils in his writings, confirms

Moffatt's testimony. Patrick's biographers confirm that he observed and taught the Sabbath of the fourth commandment.

One early biographer wrote of Patrick: "The angel was wont to come to him every seventh day of the week, and, as one man talks to another, so Patrick enjoyed the angel's counsel and conversation." The biographer also mentioned parents who sought Patrick's advice having "heard of Patrick as a man who was visited by the everlasting God every seventh day."[13]

So, based on the historical records of past centuries, two churches co-existed through the course of time before the Protestant Reformation of the sixteenth century. One church, speaking from Rome, espoused the formation of Sunday as a substitute for the Sabbath as the day of weekly worship. The other—scattered, persecuted, and nameless, yet thriving—advanced the apostolic agenda, which included the observance of the Saturday Sabbath of the fourth commandment.

Christians in great numbers were observing the seventh-day Sabbath from the first century well into the fifth century. Why was it then that the churches in Rome and Alexandria discontinued this worship practice? And why do the vast majority of Christians in the twenty-first century choose to follow the custom of Rome and Alexandria rather than that of Jerusalem and Judea—the original center of the Christian faith, made up of the immediate associates of Jesus Christ and His disciples who were observers of the fourth commandment Saturday Sabbath? Ultimately we must ask: Why does it matter?

3. The role of the Day of Pentecost. By custom, the annual Day of Pentecost was celebrated fifty days after the Jewish Passover. Jesus was crucified the day before Passover. Therefore, the Day of Pentecost, recorded in Acts 2, occurred on the first day of the week—Sunday. Some advocates for Sunday observance point to this event as the launching of a new day in place of the Sabbath in honor of the LORD's resurrection.

Was Sunday made the "LORD's day" at Pentecost? What really did happen on this momentous day in church history? Jesus Himself predicted that something special would happen on the Day of Pentecost. Yet, He did not predict that a new day of worship would be launched.

Rather, He promised the outpouring of the Holy Spirit upon the infant church—the true fulfillment of this annual feast day of Israel.

God had provided the means by which the news of a resurrected Messiah might be taken quickly and powerfully to the civilized world. In Jerusalem that day were thousands of Sabbath-observing Jews coming from distant countries and cities. At the outpouring of the Holy Spirit, the preaching of a crucified and resurrected Christ brought thousands under conviction. Minds and hearts were opened to the reality of the gospel. A stronghold of truth was being secured and expanded.

In answer to the collective query, *"What shall we do?"* the Holy Spirit spoke through the Apostle Peter: " 'Repent and let every one of you be baptized in the name of Jesus Christ for the remission of sins . . .' " (Acts 2:37, 38).

The Holy Spirit did not point to a day to honor the LORD's resurrection, but to an *event* marking the new birth of the believer—*baptism*. As a result of obeying these instructions, three thousand "who gladly received his word were baptized" (Acts 2:41). In the days that followed, five thousand more responded to the invitation to follow the resurrected Christ and were baptized (Acts 4:4).

Pentecost is remembered more for the event of *baptism* than it is for the time of the week on which it occurred. In fact, Scripture never once calls attention to the day of the week on which the outpouring of the Holy Spirit occurred. Neither does it call for observance of the first day of the week in memorial of the Day of Pentecost, even as the Bible never calls for a memorial observance of the day on which the resurrection of Jesus occurred.

Under the guidance of the Holy Spirit, the Apostle Paul elaborated on the connection between the resurrection and baptism:

Know ye not, that so many of us as were baptized into Jesus Christ were baptized into His death? Therefore we are buried with Him by baptism into death: that like as Christ was raised up from the dead by the glory of the father, even so we also should walk in newness of life. For if we have been planted together in His death, we shall be also in the likeness of His resurrection. (Romans 6:3–5)

We find Paul's statement fitting when we take into account the urgent command Jesus gave His disciples before returning to heaven: **"Go therefore and make disciples of all nations, baptizing them in the name of the Father and of the Son and of the Holy Spirit"** (Matthew 28:19).

The experience of *baptism*, which internalizes and honors the death and resurrection of Jesus in individual believers, has the endorsement of the three persons of the Godhead, but the day of the week on which the resurrection occurred does not.

Facts are stubborn things; and whatever may be our wishes, our inclinations, or the dictates of our passions, they cannot alter the state of facts and evidence. —John Adams

CHAPTER 3

The Origin of the Claim for Sunday Sacredness

Serious questions are now before us: *How is the disbanding of the Creation Sabbath in Christianity to be accounted for? Who is responsible for the commissioning of Sunday as the LORD's day? And, whom should each individual Bible believer trust as having the right to impose obligation on the human conscience?*

Catholics have a brief, but centuries old answer about the change of the Sabbath. In the *Convert's Catechism,* which has served as a teaching handbook for believers as well as inquiring observers, is this forthright response:

Q. Which is the Sabbath day?
A. Saturday is the Sabbath day.
Q. Why do we observe Sunday instead of Saturday?
A. We observe Sunday instead of Saturday because the Catholic Church, in the Council of Laodicea (A.D. 336), transferred the solemnity from Saturday to Sunday. (Rev. Peter Geiermann, *The Convert's Catechism of Catholic Doctrine*, B. Herder, St. Louis, Missouri, 1910, p. 50) (For an authoritative statement on the solemnity of the Sabbath not being transferred to Sunday, see Supporting Exhibit #2, page 154.)

This statement directs us to a decision made at the ecclesiastical Council of Laodicea (in A.D. 365 rather than A.D. 336). In Rome, by this time, Sunday observance had replaced the seventh-day Sabbath, which, since the Jewish revolt in A.D. 135, the Roman Caesars had stigmatized as being Jewish. In Canon 29 of the council, the gathering of bishops and church prelates formulated a decision regarding the fate of Christians who chose to observe the Sabbath:

> **Christians shall not Judaize and be idle on Saturday [Greek, *sabbaton*, "Sabbath"], but shall work on that day; but the LORD's day [Sunday] they shall especially honour, and, as being Christians, shall, if possible, do no work on that day. If, however, they are found Judaizing, they shall be shut out [Greek, *anathema*] from Christ.** (Translated in Charles Joseph Hefele, *A History of the Christian Councils*, T. & T. Clark, Edinburgh, 1876, vol. 2, p. 316)

Canon 29 is the first known attempt by the Church of Rome to officially obligate all Christians to observe the first day of the week under threat of being cut off from Christ by the Church. Here, history documents the human displacement of sacred, intimate time—the seventh day.

This leads us to ask: *Why would church officials need to restrict seventh-day Sabbath observance in the fourth century if Sunday observance had been initiated by the disciples or by Christ Himself in the first weeks following His resurrection and the early Christian church had universally accepted the change?* The answer must be that unusually large numbers of Christians—Gentile Christians—were still observing the seventh-day Sabbath and were loath to adopt a tradition that has no foundation in Scripture and that was promoted by a council favoring Western Christianity centered in Rome.

We should note that Canon 29 makes no claim of support from Scripture. Nor does it claim that the disciples or apostles kept Sunday as sacred. Also absent is any command from Christianity's Cornerstone—Jesus Christ. The question surfaces again: *Who has authority over divine institutions? And are not ecclesiastical leaders pledged to enthusiastically explain, guard, and protect these institutions regardless of how secular powers view them (Acts 5:29)?*

Significantly, there is no reference to the fourth commandment in Canon 29. In fact, the pronouncement that Christians "shall work on that day" (that is, on Saturday), is in direct contradiction of the

26

fourth commandment, which states: "For the seventh day is the Sabbath of the LORD your God. In it you shall do no work" (Exodus 20:10). With this in view, we recognize that Canon 29 directs Christians to profane the seventh day (Saturday), a practice that is still widespread among most of twenty-first century Christendom.

Also puzzling and perplexing are the seemingly extreme anti-Jewish sentiments of the bishops and clerics who should have been the ones to realize that the seventh-day Sabbath is not exclusively Jewish but that it is of divine origin from the Creation and that the LORD God Himself has claimed the seventh day as His "holy day" (Isaiah 58:13). Did not the attendees of the Council of Laodicea understand how contradictory it is to cut someone off from Christ for honoring the very day of which Jesus personally declared Himself to be the lord (Matthew 12:8)?

Nevertheless, Canon 29 is not the first hint of Rome's hostility toward observance of the seventh-day Sabbath. Early in the fourth century, church historian Eusebius, who was Emperor Constantine's biographer and adviser in church affairs, reported Rome's already completed transition to Sunday observance:

. . . all things whatsoever that it was duty to do on the Sabbath, these we [the church] have transferred them to the LORD's day, as being more authoritative and more highly regarded and first in rank, and more honorable than the Jewish Sabbath. (Eusebius, Bishop of Rome [310–311], *Commentary on the Psalms,* on Psalm 91 [92]: 2, 3, in J. -P. Migne, *The Patrologia Graeca,* vol. 23, col. 1172. Greek.)

Eusebius provided the first historical clue of the new doctrine of the substitution of a new day in place of the Sabbath. The substitution occurred in Rome, and Eusebius was the ecclesiastical aide to the Roman emperor whose political strategy for uniting the Empire was a merger between paganism and Christianity.

In A.D. 321, in a politically inspired move to bring the religions of the Roman Empire together, Emperor Constantine declared that no work was to be done on Sunday. This civil edict strengthened the already prevailing custom of Sunday observance and provided a rationale for Pope Sylvester (A.D. 314–335) to declare Saturday a weekly day of fasting. He hoped that the festive atmosphere of color, music, and feasting brought to the LORD's Day (Sunday) would contrast with the somber mood of the fast on Sabbath and draw Christians in the Roman Empire to abandon Saturday observance.

Pope Sylvester did not hide his contempt for the seventh day when he declared:

> **If every Sunday is to be observed joyfully by the Christians on account of the resurrection, then every Sabbath on account of the burial is to be regarded in execration [denouncing] of the Jews.** (Quoted by S. R. E. Humbert, *Adversus Graecorum Calumnias* 6, in J. -P. Migne, *The Patrologia Latina*, vol. 143, col. 937. Latin.)

Added to the Sabbath fast was a ban on all religious meetings on Saturday—even those that would include the observance of the LORD's Supper.[14] Years later, the Council of Laodicea (A.D. 365) ordered Christians to work on the seventh day and mandated that any Christian who appeared to be "sabbatizing" would be cut off from Christ.

Historian of the early church Frederick C. Conybeare has pointed out the attitude toward the Sabbath that emerged among some highly influential Christians during this time:

> **The Christians, in order to spite the Jews, very soon began to violate the sabbath; and in time substituted their Sunday for it as the day for holding the . . . assembly . . . at which the Jewish and later on the Christian Scriptures were read, and prayer and praise offered. Efforts were made in the Church sporadically, from the fourth century on, to suspend work on Sundays, but these never succeeded . . . Had the leaders of early Christian opinion been inspired by feelings of humanity, and not by mere theological hatred, they would have encouraged instead of discouraging the Jewish day of rest.** (*The Origins of Christianity*, University Books, New York, 1958, p. 157)

How the Creation Sabbath was lost

Under Roman Christianity, the Creation Sabbath appears to be lost—not so much from carelessness or neglect—but through its intentional and calculated suppression by church leadership. What the Church of Rome could not support with Scripture, she would mandate by pontifical decree. There would be no second-guessing, no turning back. A divine boundary set at the Creation had been altered, and Rome would eventually bequeath this alteration as her legacy to the peoples of the world, both secular and religious. What followed was the emergence and eventual permanent status of the Sunday LORD's Day. (For more on the historical factors that gave birth to the Sunday LORD's Day, see Supporting Exhibit #3, on page 160.)

In the decades following the Council of Laodicea, a new rationale would emerge that would give the appearance of legitimacy in doctrinal authority to the leadership of the Church of Rome, and a new voice would suggest a rationale for the divergent weekly worship day that Rome was now promoting.

It is no coincidence that Emperor Constantine's statue stands today near the entryway to St. Peter's basilica in Rome. Constantine's influence propelled Western Christianity into a position of prominence in the Empire. However, the Caesars that followed Constantine would soon fade in prominence, and the popes of Rome would readily assume the political title of the Caesars—*Pontifix Maximus*. In place of the Caesars, papal Rome would reign unhindered in defining and controlling religious and political reality on the European continent for the next millennium.

Augustine's legacy

A personage of importance to the emerging Church of Rome after the Council of Laodicea provided the philosophical argument for papal leadership; he would also unveil a new rationale to explain the church's abandonment of the seventh-day Sabbath.

That personage was Augustine (A.D. 356–440), the bishop of Hippo in North Africa, who became known as the "doctor of the Church." His ministry to the Church of Rome is still renowned for its far-reaching influence and crafty theological intrigue. Written over a period of thirteen years, Augustine's treatise *The City of*

God provided the philosophical underpinnings for the daring claim that the Church of Rome is the mediator between God and humankind. From its first dissemination under the auspices of the Church of Rome, the people accepted the dogma that the destiny of souls depends upon the Church and that the Church has the authority to define and enforce the orthodoxy of Christian teaching. The stage was now set for the Roman Church to exercise its political and ecclesiastical will under threat of excommunication.

Augustine also provided Rome's representatives with a new theological rationale for explaining why the Sabbath had disappeared from practice. While disregarding the historical significance of the Sabbath as the seventh day in weekly time, Augustine reasoned that the "Old Law" Sabbath, like the ceremonial laws, had been replaced by a "New Law"—existential experience of rest from sin in the heart. Here are his words:

> **God proclaims to us a Sabbath. What sort of Sabbath? First consider, where it is. It is in the heart, within us; for many are idle with their limbs, while they are disturbed in conscience. . . . That very joy in the tranquility of our hope, is our Sabbath. This is the subject of praise and of song in this Psalm, how a Christian man is in the Sabbath of his own heart, that is, in the quiet, tranquility, and serenity of his conscience, undisturbed; hence he tells us here, whence men are wont to be disturbed, and he teaches thee to keep Sabbath in thine own heart.** (Augustine, *On the Psalms*, Philip Schaff, editor, *A Select Library of the Nicene and Post-Nicene Fathers of the Christian Church*, series 1, vol. 8, Hendrickson, Peabody, Massachusetts, 1994, p. 453)

With these words, Augustine dislodged the Sabbath from its foundation in Creation and spiritualized the fourth commandment into a metaphor.

One hundred fifty years after Augustine, in a letter to the Roman people, Pope Gregory the Great (590–604) denounced those who maintained that no one should work on the seventh day. He called those who continued to support Sabbath observance "prophets of

Antichrist." Pope Gregory asserted that the Sabbath cannot be reinstated without restoring the whole ceremonial system. Disregarding the Creation Sabbath as "sacred time," he dismissed the seventh day with the spiritualization—"Christ is our Sabbath" (James T. Ringgold, *Sunday: Legal Aspects of the First Day of the Week*, Frederick D. Linn & Company, Jersey City, 1891, p. 267).

Through the centuries, others, such as Thomas Aquinas, John Calvin and several modern proponents of worship on Sunday, have attempted to label the Sabbath as temporary and ceremonial in nature. But all such attempts have failed to answer the following far-reaching questions: *Why did the Creator give the seventh day in the weekly cycle as a blessing to humans at the Creation before the entrance of sin? Why did God not tell the apostles and the infant Christian church about this change or record it in Sacred Writ? Why do historians find nearly the whole of early Christianity vibrantly observing the historic seventh-day Sabbath of which Jesus said He was LORD? And why would God have associated the words "perpetual" and "forever" with the Sabbath covenant at Mt. Sinai (Exodus 31:13–17)?* Do these questions not negate any attempt to label the Sabbath as "temporary" or "ceremonial"?

Regardless of the several attempts of prominent Catholic theologians to explain and legitimize the first day of the week as the Christian day of worship, Catholic leaders through the centuries have primarily based their claims for the legitimacy of the change from Saturday to Sunday upon one factor—the ecclesiastical authority of the papacy.

Since early medieval times, Catholics have alleged that the papal ecclesiastical system has the on-going authority to augment Scripture in matters of church practice and teaching. We close this chapter with Keenan's *Doctrinal Catechism*, which is one Catholic pronouncement among several that has reference to the issue of the change of the Sabbath:

Q.—Have you any other way of proving that the Church has power to institute festivals of precept?
A.—Had she not such power, she could not have done that in which all modern religionists agree with her;—she could not have substituted the observance of Sunday, the first day

of the week, for the observance of Saturday, the seventh day, a change for which there is no Scriptural authority. (Rev. Stephen Keenan, A *Doctrinal Catechism; Wherein Divers Points of Catholic Faith and Practice Assailed by Modern Heretics Are Sustained by an Appeal to the Holy Scriptures, the Testimony of the Ancient Fathers, and the Dictates of Reason on the Basis of Scheffmacher's Catechism*, J. P. Kenedy and Sons, New York, 1846, p. 174)

Prove all things; hold fast that which is good.
—The Apostle Paul (1 Thessalonians 5:21)

CHAPTER 4
The Protestant Dilemma

Many of today's Protestant leaders question the accuracy of Rome's claim to have changed the day of weekly worship to Sunday. Did they not do so, these leaders would have to admit that the change of the Sabbath is based on a human action rather than on the foundation of inspired Scripture.

However, in their reluctance to recognize the historical role of the Church of Rome in this matter, they must willfully overlook the words of their Protestant forefathers of the sixteenth century, for, in the first draft of the Augsburg Confession of 1530, German Reformer Philipp Melanchthon gave this reason for separating from the Church of Rome:

> **So one may also observe, that the Sabbath was changed to Sunday against the Ten Commandments, for which they [the Catholic Church] consider it, and no example is held so high and vaunted so much, as the change of the Sabbath, and wish therewith to maintain the significance of the power of the church because it has tampered with the Ten Commandments and changed something therein.** (*Kirchen-Gesangbuch für Evangelisch-Lutherische Gemeinden ungeänderter Augsburgischer Confession,* Lutherischer concordia Verliag, St. Louis, Missouri, 1886; p. 405. German. Translated by Gideon D. Hagstotz, PhD, and Hilda B. Hagstotz, PhD, *Heroes of the Reformation,* Pacific Press Publishing Assoc., Mountain View, Calif., 1951, p. 171)

Philipp Melanchthon was the younger contemporary and trusted associate of Martin Luther. His personal demeanor and scholarly ability gave him far-reaching influence and favor with the Reformation leaders in Germany. Melanchthon was the person chosen to present the Confession before the court of Emperor Charles V. It is unlikely that he would have thought to include this statement regarding the Church of Rome's claims had they not been widely known and affirmed by his colleagues.

Fine-tuned for the final draft, the German Reformers' Confession, article 28, gives official voice to a key reason for their separation from the Church of Rome—a church, as they claimed, that had gone outside the parameters of Scripture for its doctrine and practice. (See Supporting Exhibit #4, on page 162.) This is their historic statement:

> **. . . they [the Catholics] appeal to the fact that the Sabbath was changed to Sunday—contrary, as they say, to the Ten Commandments. No case is appealed to and urged so insistently as the change of the Sabbath, for thereby they wish to maintain that the power of the church is indeed great because the church has dispensed from and altered part of the Ten Commandments.** (John H. Leith, *Creeds of the Churches: A Reader in Christian Doctrine from the Bible to the Present*, Doubleday & Company, Inc., Garden City, New York, 1963, pp. 100, 101)

The Protestant platform challenge

The Reformers had restored a long-lost standard. Cochlaeus, a Catholic writer of the time, referred to it: "Luther had persuaded his followers to put no faith in any other oracle than the Holy Scriptures."[15] Sixteenth century Protestant Reformers, including Martin Luther, based their religious beliefs on *sola scriptura*, which is Latin for "the Bible only." They were declaring Scripture to be the authoritative standard in deciding matters of Christian faith and practice. The Reformers enlarged on this slogan with the Latin phrase, *scriptura sui ipsius intepres; scripturam ex scritura explicandam esse,* which conveys the concept that the Bible is its own interpreter and that teachers of essential spiritual truths do not need help from non-biblical sources, such as human reasoning, tradition, philosophy, or the church.

The Bible is in a class all its own—that of sacred, inspired canon (2 Peter 1:19–21).

A weakness in application

But there was a weakness in the Protestant application of this position, one that Catholic debaters of the time exploited.

Dr. Johann Eck, assistant to the Archbishop of Trier in southwestern Germany, challenged Luther to debate the authority of the papal system as it related to the authority of Scripture. He knew very well that Scripture did not support the observance of Sunday and that the practice of keeping Sunday was a result of Catholic tradition.

Disputing with Luther, Dr. Eck articulated the Protestant dilemma:

If, however, the Church has had power to change the Sabbath of the Bible into Sunday and to command Sunday-keeping, why should it not have also the power concerning other days, many of which are based on Scripture—such as Christmas, circumcision of the heart, three kings, etc. If you omit the latter, and turn from the church to the Scriptures alone, then you must keep the Sabbath with the Jews, which has been kept from the beginning of the world. (*Enchiridion*, Wießenhorn, Augsburg, 1533, p. 190. German.)

Dr. Eck had struck a tender nerve; he had located a loose plank in the Protestant platform, which other Catholic debaters would exploit, as well, against Protestant foes. Since then, this persistent question continues to confront the thinking of every Sunday-observing Protestant: *Will I obligate my conscience to Catholic tradition or will I obligate it to the Bible?*

Eck was defending the authority of the Church of Rome to determine religious doctrine and practice. How have other Catholic leaders through the centuries viewed the papal system? A Catholic author notably wrote:

1. The Pope is of so great dignity and so exalted he is not a mere man, but as it were God, and the vicar of God. . .

30. The Pope can modify divine law, since his power is not of man but of God, and he acts as vicegerent of God upon earth with most ample power of binding and loosing his sheep. . . . (Translated from the original Latin of the eighteenth-century Roman Catholic Lucius Ferraris, article 2, "Papa" *Prompta bibliotheca, canonica, juridica, moralis, theologica nec non ascetica, polemica, rubricistica, historica*, J. -P. Migne, Paris, 1858, vol. 5, col. 1823. Latin.)

The Roman *Decretalia,* a work on Roman ecclesiastical law, details the powers that the Roman Catholic Church ascribes to the pope:

He can pronounce sentences and judgments in contradiction to the right of nations, to the law of God and man. . . He can free himself from the commands of the apostles, he being their superior, and from the rules of the Old Testament, &c.

The pope has power to change times, to abrogate laws, and to dispense with all things, even the precepts of Christ. (Gloss to *Decretales Domini Gregori IX,* Lib 1, Title vii, "DE TRANSLATIONE EPISCOPI" ["On the Transference of Bishops"], cap. 3, "Quanto," quoted in *Collection of Facts for the Times,* 1875, p. 137; cited in *The Acts and Monuments of John Fox,* 1837, vol. 4, p. 159; and the latter part quoted in *The American Textbook of Popery: Being an Authentic Compend of the Bulls, Canons, and Decretals of the Roman Hierarchy*, Griffith & Simon, Philadelphia, 1847, p. 210)

An echo through time

Following the debate in the summer of 1519, Eck was invited to Rome, where Pope Leo X ordained him as the papal legate in recognition of his skillful defense of the Church. His challenge to Protestants regarding *sola scriptura* continues to echo through the centuries to our day.

In his best-selling polemic book written especially for non-Catholic readers, *The Faith of Millions,* Father John A. O'Brien repeats Eck's line of thought:

But since Saturday, not Sunday, is specified in the Bible, isn't it curious that non-Catholics who profess to take their religion directly from the Bible and not from the Church, observe Sunday instead of Saturday? Yes, of course, it is inconsistent; but this change was made about fifteen centuries before Protestantism was born, and by that time the custom was universally observed. They have continued the custom [of Sunday observance], even though it rests upon the authority of the Catholic Church and not upon an explicit text in the Bible. That observance remains as a reminder of the Mother Church from which the non-Catholic sects broke away—like a boy running away from home but still carrying in his pocket a picture of his mother or a lock of her hair. (*The Faith of Millions*, Our Sunday Visitor Inc. Huntington, Indiana, 1974, pp. 400, 401)

Again, in remarkable directness, president of Redemptorist College in Kansas City, Missouri, Roman Catholic Priest Timothy Enright passionately explained in a public letter the role his church has played in this matter:

Prove to me from the Bible alone that I am bound to keep Sunday holy. There is no such law in the Bible. It is a law of the holy Catholic Church alone. The Bible says "Remember the Sabbath day to keep it holy." The Catholic Church says, No. By my divine power I abolish the Sabbath day and command you to keep holy the first day of the week. And Lo! the entire civilized world bows down in reverent obedience to the command of the holy Catholic Church. (In a lecture at Hartford, Kansas, February 18, 1884, and printed in the Hartford, Kansas, *Weekly Call,* February 22, 1884, and *The American Sentinel* [a Roman Catholic journal in New York], June, 1893, p. 173)

CHAPTER 5
The Catholic Dilemma

M artin Luther and Johann Eck were the two finest theologians in all of Germany in the sixteenth century. Luther was summoned to stand before Emperor Charles V in April, 1521, at the Diet of Worms, to defend his beliefs that conflicted with Catholic Church teachings.

Eck was selected to be the prosecuting spokesman for the Emperor. Before the gathered church dignitaries, princes, spectators and the Emperor himself, Eck called upon Martin Luther to denounce and retract his writings. This was a momentous and suspenseful moment in church history.

Eck, who chose to draw his beliefs from the treasury of Catholic tradition, and Luther, who drew his from the bedrock of Scripture alone, represent the two streams that form Christianity today— Catholic and Protestant.

This is the dilemma that all Catholics—all people really—have had before them through the centuries and to our day: *When the tradition of the Church conflicts with Scripture, to which will I choose to obligate my conscience?*

Jesus said of Himself: " 'I am the way, the *truth,* and the life" (John 14:6, emphasis supplied). He also stated: " 'Your word is *truth*" (John 17:17, emphasis supplied). When He faced His adversary in the wilderness, He answered the adversary's temptation with the words, "It is written, 'man shall not live by bread alone, but by every word that proceeds from the mouth of God' " (Matthew 4:4). Jesus was setting a precedent that His believers and teachers should follow in deciding matters of faith.

So, regarding the keeping of Sunday as the day of worship, we ask: What *has* "proceeded from the mouth of God" in His Word? Prominent Catholic leader James Cardinal Gibbons (1834–1921) of Baltimore wrote:

> **. . . is not every Christian obliged to sanctify Sunday and to abstain on that day from unnecessary servile work? Is not the observance of this law among the most prominent of our sacred duties? But you may read the Bible from Genesis to Revelation, and you will not find a single line authorizing the sanctification of Sunday. The Scriptures enforce the religious observance of Saturday, a day which we never sanctify. . . . We must, therefore, conclude that the Scriptures *alone* cannot be a sufficient guide and rule of faith."** (*The Faith of Our Fathers*, John Murphy Co., Baltimore, 1876, 1920, p. 89)

Cardinal Gibbons has rightly concluded that there is not a line in Scripture from the mouth of God regarding Sunday sacredness. We are left to assume the Cardinal is leaving the reader to look to a human ecclesiastical source for this religious practice.

What, then, *has* " 'proceeded from the mouth of God' " regarding the seventh day?

In a thunderous "shock and awe" event at Mt. Sinai fourteen hundred years before the birth of Jesus, the Creator God audibly spoke the fourth commandment to the attentive ears of two million freed slaves in the desert (Exodus 19:16–25; 20:1–26). All trembled with respect at His majesty and awesome presence. They were the Israelite nation, whom God was preparing to communicate His commandments, His mercy, and His character to a wayward world. Through Israel God had purposed to bring the nations of the planet into redeeming fellowship with the Living God. The Israelites were not being called to exclusiveness, but to exemplify—to parade before the world—the benefits of holiness to the LORD.

Soon after, the LORD instructed Moses to place the Ten Commandment tables of stone, which He Himself had inscribed, into the most secure treasure box on earth—the gold-laden Ark of the Covenant kept within the Most Holy Place of the LORD's tabernacle. There the Shekinah glory, the visible manifestation of the Creator God, glowed brilliantly between the cherubim and above the mercy seat that covered all of the commandments, including the fourth—which God had specifically declared to be "perpetual" and to last "forever" (Exodus 31:16, 17).

Later, Moses wrote that he had received this order from the Sovereign of the universe:

"You shall not add to the word which I command you, nor take anything from it, that you may keep the commandments of the LORD your God which I command you." (Deuteronomy 4:2; see also Proverbs 30:5, 6)

And fourteen hundred years later, Jesus publicly reinforced this directive: " 'For assuredly, I say to you, till heaven and earth shall pass away, one jot or one tittle will by no means pass from the law [which includes the fourth commandment] till all is fulfilled' " (Matthew 5:18). How, then, would anyone dare to alter as much as one word? Who would ever think to suggest a substitute? Who would say it is only a trivial, insignificant matter?

The Ten Commandments are of the highest heavenly order. Paul declared that the Ten Commandments are "holy, just, and good" (Romans 7:12). King David referred to the Law as "perfect, converting the soul" (Psalm 19:7). James described the law for the person of faith as the "law of liberty" (James 2:12). The Author of the commandments declared the Sabbath of the fourth commandment "blessed" and "holy." The commandments are cosmic moral high ground—they embody the point of reference for the conscience of every person on earth. The Ten Commandment law is a revealing of the very essence of God's nature. This is why the tablets of stone were given a foundational position within the Ark of the Covenant. To alter this divine description of the righteous God would be to change the very nature of His righteous being.

Does tampering with the fourth commandment, even by high-ranking clerics, call for the same sentence as that pronounced for violating the book of Revelation? Here are John's words:

If anyone adds to these things, God will add to him the plagues that are written in this book: and if anyone takes away from the words of this prophecy, God shall take away his part in the Book of Life, from the holy city and from the things which are written in this book. (Revelation 22:18, 19)

On this point, you must make the call.

*For the word of God. . . is a discerner of the
thoughts and intents of the heart.*
—The Apostle Paul (Hebrews 4:12)

CHAPTER 6
Primacy—Scripture or Church Tradition?

In a statement quoted above, Catholic spokesman Cardinal Gibbons laid out the Catholic position: "We must, therefore, conclude that the Scriptures alone cannot be a sufficient guide and rule of faith."

Catholic apologists have maintained that Christianity has a "living teacher" and that the Church receives continuing authoritative direction in practice and doctrine through the magisterium—"the pope and the bishops in communion with him." This is the basis upon which the Catholic Church claims that Sunday can replace the Sabbath.

The Church of Rome has consistently taught that the magisterium is the only authoritative interpreter of Scripture:

> **For all of what has been said about the way of interpreting Scripture is subject finally to the judgment of the Church, which carries out the divine commission and ministry of guarding and interpreting the word of God.** ("Dei verbum," *The Documents of Vatican II,* Walter M. Abbott, ed., New York, 1966, p. 121 [2.3.12], in William A. Van Roo, *Basics of a Roman Catholic Theology,* p. 146.)

According to Pope Gregory VII, who governed the church in the eleventh century, with reference to faith and morals, he stated: ". . . the Roman church has never erred and never will err till the end of time" (Robert McClory, *Power and the Papacy*, p. 19).

What level of importance, then, does the magisterium place on Sunday observance, even though, by its own admission, the practice is not supported by Scripture? A recent catechism explains:

The Sunday celebration of the LORD's Day and his Eucharist [Mass] is at the heart of the Church's life. (*Catechism of the Catholic Church*, Doubleday, New York, 1994, p. 582)

Ever since Protestants came into being more than five hundred years ago with the claim that "Scripture alone" ought to determine Christian faith and practice, the focus of authority has been the central issue of separation between the Catholic and Protestant streams of Christianity.

Is there a "rule of faith" beyond Scripture that must "obligate the conscience" of every Christian, even if it conflicts with Scripture?

Moreover, are the Ten Commandments to be considered a "living document," subject to human alteration to accommodate changing societal circumstances and preferences?

Has God authorized clerics to modify the very code by which all will be judged (James 2:12)?

King David, who lived a thousand years before Christ, wrote: "Concerning Your testimonies [the Commandments], I have known of old that You have founded them forever" (Psalms 119:152).

After Paul preached the gospel in Berea, those who heard him went to the Scriptures to test the truthfulness of what he said. Luke reported, "These were more fair-minded than those in Thessalonica, in that they received the word with all readiness, and searched the Scriptures daily to find out whether these things were so" (Acts 17:11).

When confronting the religious elite who had also placed man-made beliefs above the Old Testament Scriptures, Jesus queried:

" 'Why do you also transgress the commandment of God because of your tradition? . . . Hypocrites! Well did Isaiah prophesy about you saying: . . . in vain they worship me, teaching as doctrines the commandments of men' " (Matthew 15:3, 7, 8).

Pope Leo X excommunicated Luther as a heretic in January, 1521. This meant that Luther's writings, preaching and teaching were then outlawed. He was summoned to appear before Emperor Charles V several months later at the Diet of Worms. In coming to Worms, Luther had expected that the Emperor would give him the opportunity to defend his writings before the princes and prelates. Unfortunately, however, he was abruptly ordered to come to the point: would he retract his allegedly heretical writings? The Emperor had the power to carry out his execution. Facing the most august dignitaries in the empire, Luther answered both in German and in Latin:

I cannot submit my faith either to the pope or to the councils, because it is clear as the day that they have frequently erred and contradicted each other. Unless therefore I am convinced by the testimony of Scripture or by the clearest reasoning, unless I am persuaded by means of the passages I have quoted, and unless they thus render my conscience bound by the Word of God, I cannot and I will not retract, for it is unsafe for a Christian to speak against his conscience. Here I stand, I can do no other; may God help me! Amen! (J. H. Merle d'Aubigné, *History of the Reformation of the Sixteenth Century,* bk. 7, chap. 8)

Martin Luther's answer to the Emperor and his illustrious audience was delivered with a calmness, dignity and self-command that surprised everyone and disappointed his enemies. Many were convinced that a divine influence surrounded him, and they were moved to more firmly defend the justness of his cause.

Further attempts at Worms to bring Luther to compromise with Rome were answered with these words—

I consent with all my heart, that the emperor, the princes, and even the meanest Christian, should examine and judge my works; but on one condition, that they take the Word of God for their standard. Men have nothing to do but to obey it. Do not offer violence to my conscience, which is bound and chained up with the Holy Scriptures. (d'Aubigne, *History of the Reformation of the Sixteenth Century,* bk. 7, chap. 10)

At the conclusion of the Diet, the representatives of the pope urged the Emperor to seize Luther in order that he might be put to the same fate as that of John Huss one hundred years earlier. However, Charles V chose rather to honor the safe passage he had promised the professor from Wittenberg. Without compromising Scripture and violating his conscience, Martin Luther had bravely faced death.

In the course of time, momentous events often turn the tide and chart the course of humanity for generations to follow. Luther's appearance at the Diet of Worms did this for Protestantism. This confrontation between emperor and heretic, which would become the most significant event of the century, became for many people the pivotal moment that energized and propelled the reform movement into a permanent spiritual force in the religious world.

Another significant event soon followed that would do the same for Catholicism. However, the impact of this event and the surprising issue that brought it to its conclusion is far less known and appreciated. Yet, its consequence becomes an opportunity for choice in every succeeding generation.

When Christianity takes the name of Christ but does not live by His teachings, it loses its authority.
—Alejandro Bullón

CHAPTER 7
The Archbishop of Reggio

During the sixteenth century, the Reformers throughout Europe were bringing many fresh Bible insights out into the open, exposing the unbiblical traditions and spiritual error that had accumulated over the centuries. This challenged the Church of Rome to look at itself and correct its course. How would she respond?

As the Bible-based reforms of the Protestant Reformers began to appeal to increasingly larger portions of the populace, Catholic leaders began to agitate resistance against the Reformers.

In 1546, the year before Luther's death, Catholic bishops, cardinals, legates and church dignitaries converged on the town of Treno in the mountains of northern Italy. The prestigious Council of Trent that then began would be in and out of session for eighteen years. The decisions that were made there formed the basis of the Catholic Counter Reformation.

The turning point that would set the course for Catholic Church philosophy for coming generations came on March 16, 1562, with a unanimous vote during the council's seventeenth session. A Catholic source described the mood leading to this momentous event:

There was a strong party even of the Catholics within the council who were in favor of abandoning tradition and adopting *the Scriptures only,* as the standard of authority. This view was so decidedly held in the debates in the council that the pope's legates actually wrote to him that there was "a strong tendency to set aside tradition altogether and

to make Scriptures the soul standard of appeal." But to do this would manifestly be to go a long way toward justifying the claims of the Protestants. By this crisis there was devolved upon the ultra-Catholic portion of the council the task of convincing the others that *"Scripture and tradition"* were the only sure ground to stand upon. (*The Catholic Mirror,* Baltimore, Maryland, September 23, 1893, emphasis supplied)

This question was debated day after day. At a crucial point in the debate, the Archbishop of Reggio, Gaspar de Fosso, gave an impassioned speech that turned the tide of thinking for the entire assembly. This was the Archbishop's unusual twist of reasoning:

Such is the condition of the heretics of this age that on nothing do they rely more than that, under the pretense of the word of God, they overthrow the authority of the church; as though the church, His body could be opposed to the word of Christ, or the head to the body. On the contrary, the authority of the church, then, is illustrated most clearly by the Scriptures; for while on the one hand she recommends them, declares them to be divine, offers them to us to be read, in doubtful matters explains them faithfully, and condemns whatever is contrary to them; on the other hand, the legal precepts in the Scriptures taught by the LORD have ceased by virtue of the same authority. The Sabbath, the most glorious day in the law, has been changed into the LORD's day. . . . These and other similar matters have not ceased by virtue of Christ's teaching (for He says He has come to fulfill the law, not to destroy it), but they have been changed by the authority of the church. (Address in the 17th session of the Council of Trent, January 18, 1562, in Mansi, *Sacrorum Conciliorum,* vol. 33, cols. 529, 530, Latin.)

Archbishop Reggio urged upon the assembly the primary foundation upon which the Church of Rome had been built—*tradition.* And the delegates to the council realized that though the Protestants probably wouldn't have admitted it, by one position they held, they were acknowledging the authority of the Church. Though they claimed to base their doctrines on "the Bible and the Bible only" (*sola scriptura*), their claim didn't stand up because of their observance of Sunday. If the Reformers truly believed Scripture to be the only source of spiritual authority, they would have observed the seventh day as commanded in God's law. But by their continued observance of Sunday, they showed their recognition of the tradition authorized by the Church against Scripture.

The response to the Archbishop's appeal was immediate. The editor of *The Catholic Mirror* observed:

The argument was hailed in the council as of Inspiration only; the party for "Scripture alone," surrendered; and the council at once unanimously condemned Protestantism and the whole Reformation as only an unwarranted revolt from the communion and authority of the Catholic church. (*The Catholic Mirror*, September 23, 1893)

The *Catholic Mirror* editor also noted the primary factor in the council's decision to affirm: "Scripture and tradition are to be received and venerated equally." He said:

. . . in this vital controversy, the key, the chiefest and cumulative expression, of the Protestant inconsistency, was in the rejection of the Sabbath of the LORD, the seventh day, enjoined in the Scriptures, and the adoption and observance of the Sunday as enjoined by the Catholic church. (*The Catholic Mirror*, September 23, 1893)

We might ask, if Scripture and tradition are to be treated equally, which one should be trusted the most when there is a conflict between the two? Note this curious answer:

The Bible still teaches that the Sabbath or Saturday should be kept holy. There is no authority in the New Testament for the substitution of Sunday for Saturday. Surely it is an

important matter. **It stands there in the Bible as one of the Ten Commandments of God. There is no authority in the Bible for abrogating this Commandment, or for transferring its observance to another day of the week . . .** *The Church is above the Bible,* **and this transference of Sabbath observance is proof of that fact.** (*The Catholic Record,* September 1, 1923, vol. XLV, no. 2342, 4, emphasis supplied)

Catholics often seem to be in the precarious position of having to choose between loyalty to the tradition of the church and faithfulness to the Scriptures.

In 1998, in his notable apologetic Encyclical on Sunday Sacredness, *Dies Domini,* Pope John Paul II made this curious statement:

Christ came to accomplish a new "exodus," to restore freedom to the oppressed. He performed many healings on the Sabbath (cf. Mt 12:9–14 and parallels), certainly not to violate the LORD's Day, but to reveal its full meaning: "The Sabbath was made for man, not man for the Sabbath" (Mk 2:27). Opposing the excessive legalistic interpretation of some of his contemporaries, and developing the true meaning of the biblical Sabbath, Jesus, as "LORD of the Sabbath" (Mk 2:28), restores to the Sabbath observance its liberating character, carefully safeguarding the rights of God and the rights of human beings. This is why Christians, called as they are to proclaim the liberation won by the blood of Christ, felt that they had the authority to transfer the meaning of the Sabbath to the day of the Resurrection. (Pope John Paul II, *Dies Domini,* May 31, 1998).

To his credit, Pope John Paul II rightfully asserted Jesus' mission of magnifying the fourth commandment and bringing renewed honor and meaning to it. John Paul has also rightfully called the seventh-day Sabbath that Jesus kept the "LORD's day." Protestants who ascribe to authentic *sola scriptura* can heartily agree.

However, in the closing line of the thought, the Pope has introduced a puzzling twist in the rationale for the transfer of the "meaning of the Sabbath" to Sunday. He wrote that Christians, "called as they are to proclaim the liberation won by the blood of Christ, felt that they had the authority to transfer the meaning of the Sabbath to the day of the Resurrection."

While John Paul II, no doubt, was well meaning, is his reasoning not misguided? Does the "liberation won by the blood of Christ" entitle the body of believers to alter the wisdom of the ages—to change sacred time? Is it not the LORD's prerogative, as Head of the church, to designate holy time? And what about Jesus' specific statements that humans should not change what He has commanded (Deuteronomy 4:2; Matthew 5:18)? I hear the familiar crinkle of the pages of my Bible as I reread these verses. And I am left puzzled—*have these directives from Jesus Christ been lost to the Christian world? Is Holy Writ so easily overridden?*

The Council of Trent declared, "Scripture and tradition are to be received and venerated equally." However, in practice the Church appears to elevate one over the other. Since, in this case, there is a contradiction between church tradition and the Scripture, the Catholic reader must choose between church tradition and the Bible. Again, which will the reader allow to obligate his or her conscience?

Is there a reason why Catholic leaders, including the late Pope John Paul II, have so decisively acted as guardians and promoters of Sunday observance throughout the centuries? Cardinal Gibbons gave this clue:

> **Of course the Catholic Church claims that the change [of the Sabbath] was her act. It could not have been otherwise, as none in those days would have dreamed of doing anything in matters spiritual and ecclesiastical and religious without her. And the act is a *mark of her ecclesiastical power and authority* in religious matters.** (In a letter to J. F. Snyder of Bloomington, Illinois from C. F. Thomas, Chancellor for James Cardinal Gibbons, November 11, 1895, emphasis supplied)

With this information in mind, we must ask: *Should you be content with a Christian church declaring itself above Scripture?*

And is it not true that Protestants in the twenty-first century, by their continuing Sunday observance, are yet showing allegiance to Rome's declared authority? Or is the Protestant Reformation unfinished; and will it yet advance to fully embrace the principle of *sola scriptura*?

Ultimately, whether Catholic or Protestant or simply a believer in Christ, who will we allow to have the "right to impose obligation on the conscience"?

History is not history unless it is the truth.
—Abraham Lincoln

CHAPTER 8
A Protestant Version of Sunday Sacredness

As we have seen, Catholics claim that the Roman Catholic Church has the authority to transfer the Sabbath's sacredness to Sunday. What explanation do today's Protestants give for their acceptance of that switch?

As we have previously noted, in theory, Protestants seek to shape their understanding of God's will and Christian practice straight from the Bible, which they believe to inherently posses the inspired authorship of God (2 Peter 1:19–21). Many Protestants would answer positively to this guiding theorem: "Because the Bible is God's book, it comes to us with God's full, absolute and binding authority."[16]

For a Protestant under the authority of Scripture, a change in the observance of the day of worship must be linked directly to Jesus Himself and to the inspired writers of the New Testament. After all, a change in sacred time denotes an alteration in the expressed will of God at the very highest level—that of moral law, of which the fourth commandment is a part. The commandment declares:

Remember the Sabbath day, to keep it holy. Six days you shall labor and do all your work, but the seventh day is the Sabbath of the LORD your God. In it you shall do no work. . . For in six days the LORD made the heavens and the earth, the sea, and all that is in them and rested the seventh day. Therefore the LORD blessed the Sabbath day and hallowed it. (Exodus 20:8–11)

Along with marriage between one man and one woman, the Saturday Sabbath is uniquely tied to the Garden of Eden. In unbroken cycle from God's rest in Creation week and declared by God centuries later at Sinai to be "perpetual and eternal," it received this pronouncement by Jesus: " 'For the Son of Man is LORD even of the Sabbath' " (Matthew 12:8).

Here, then, is how the divinely established day of worship from Creation was allegedly changed, as explained by the late Dr. D. James Kennedy, founding pastor of the Coral Ridge Presbyterian Church in Fort Lauderdale, Florida, and founder and late President of John Knox Theological Seminary:

For millennia, Jews set aside the seventh day for worship. After Jesus' resurrection, Jewish followers of Christ suddenly began to worship on the first day of the week. Why? Nothing other than the Resurrection, a monumental event that took place on the first day of the week, can account for this rapid alteration from such a long and tenaciously held belief. (Dr. D. James Kennedy, *Impact* newsletter, April 2003, p. 8)

Countless numbers of God-fearing Protestant Christians who observe Sunday sacredness hold views similar to those of Dr. Kennedy. This includes several well-known Protestant apologists.[17]

Obviously, this claim is quite different from the one made by the Roman Catholic Church. However, the Protestants who hold Kennedy's view need to answer the question, *In studying early Christian church history, have you found this description of the early days of the Christian church to be authentic? Did Jewish followers of Christ "suddenly" begin to worship on the first day of the week? Was there really a "rapid alteration" from Sabbath observance to Sunday worship following the resurrection of Jesus?*

We must ask why it is that Protestant apologists cannot reference Dr. Kennedy's account with even one historically viable source, to say nothing of the Bible. The writings of the early church fathers contain no claims that Sunday observance was mandated or practiced by the apostles and disciples during the first century of this era.

Furthermore, historians confirm that a great many Jewish and Gentile Christians were still observing the seventh-day Sabbath five hundred years beyond the resurrection of Jesus. M. Max B. Turner, professor of New Testament Studies at the London School of Theology, confirmed the absence of evidence:

We must conclude that it is barely imaginable that first-day Sabbath observance commenced before the Jerusalem council. Nor can we stop there; we must go on to maintain that first-day Sabbath observance cannot easily be understood as a phenomenon of the apostolic age or of apostolic authority at all. (*From Sabbath to* LORD's *Day: A Biblical, Historical, and Theological Investigation*, Zondervan, Grand Rapids, Michigan, 1982, D. A. Carson, editor, pp. 135–136)

Evidence about the first followers of Jesus

One strategically placed but easily missed detail in the Gospel of Luke gives an important clue as to whether or not the early church abandoned the seventh-day Sabbath. Luke, a physician and the only Gentile author whose writings are preserved in the New Testament, wrote to another Gentile, whom he identified as "most excellent Theophilus," to give him "certainty in the things in which he was instructed" (Luke 1:1–4). Almost thirty years after the day of Jesus' crucifixion, Luke wrote:

That day was the Preparation, and the Sabbath drew near. And the women who had come with Him [Jesus] from Galilee followed after, and they observed the tomb and how His body was laid. Then they returned and prepared spices and fragrant oils. And they rested on the Sabbath *according to the commandment* (Luke 23:54–56, emphasis supplied).

Here, the Gentile writer Luke shows that the fourth commandment was very much alive and respected by Gentiles even thirty years after the founding of the Christian church. Furthermore, Luke's Gospel makes no mention of the resurrection being a rationale for a new day of worship. Instead, he states the reason the women rested—because of "the commandment," and he takes for granted that his

54

Gentile reader will understand exactly which "commandment" he meant.

Another New Testament clue—subdued, yet surprising and relevant to the point—is found in the story of the death of the deacon Stephen. Three years after the resurrection of Jesus, Stephen was arrested and brought before the Sanhedrin on false charges. This stalwart teacher of the gospel made a noble defense (in Acts 7). Of the charges brought against him, none related to Stephen's abandoning the Sabbath law of the Jews. He was condemned and stoned to death for his unwavering faithfulness to the resurrected LORD Jesus Christ, not for violating the Creation Sabbath or for leading others to do so.

As a henchman of the Sanhedrin, Saul relentlessly persecuted the infant church. Yet, never did he harass and kill Jewish believers on the charge of abandoning the Sabbath and instituting another day in its place to honor the resurrection of Jesus.

Some time after his conversion, Saul became the Christian Paul. During his ministry as the apostle to the Gentiles, Paul was continually dogged by representatives of the Pharisees for not practicing circumcision and other ceremonial customs. Yet, never was he accused of abandoning observance of the fourth commandment Sabbath for that of the first day. His later defense before Roman governor Festus is especially revealing. He said: " 'Neither against the law of the Jews, nor against the temple, nor against Caesar have I offended in anything at all' " (Acts 25:8).

Paul's exposition of the Resurrection theme, in First Corinthians chapter 15, is rich and far-reaching. The absence in that exposition of any reference to a Sunday celebration of the Resurrection is glaring. He calls the day of the resurrection merely "the third day" (1 Corinthians 15:4).

Fourth century historian Epiphanius provides another clue about weekly worship practices of Jewish followers of Jesus in Judea in the first century. He wrote that those Jewish Christians who fled Jerusalem prior to its destruction in A.D. 70 were all observers of the seventh-day Sabbath (*Panarion*, sect 29, chap. 7, verses 5, 7, 8). In this light, we can consider what Jesus intended when He warned His disciples regarding the fate of Jerusalem: " 'And pray that your flight may not be in winter or on the Sabbath' " (Matthew 24:20). We can deduce from Jesus' statement that He did not expect His followers to cease observing the weekly Sabbath within the New Covenant era.

Jerusalem was the initial center of first century Christianity. Its spirit and practice was the model for church planting in the Gentile territories. The followers of Jesus among the Jews set an example in suffering, persecution, and sacrifice for the sake of Christ. Therefore, it is no small commendation when the Apostle Paul wrote to the fledgling and mostly Gentile church in Thessalonica: "For you, brethren, became imitators of the churches of God which are in Judea in Christ Jesus. For you also suffered the same things from your own countrymen, just as they did from the Jews . . ." (1 Thessalonians 2:14). While Paul does not specifically mention Sabbath observance, it was certainly a significant practice of the Jewish believers. With the Sabbath-observing Jewish Christian churches in Judea being the original pattern for the early church in practice, experience and doctrine, we must ask if the first century Judean church model mentioned by Paul is still worthy of imitation by followers of Jesus in the twenty-first century.

Finally, the words of Jesus have a bearing on this question. From the "Sermon on the Mount"—the explanation of the principles of the kingdom of heaven—Jesus said: " 'Do not think that I have come to destroy the Law or the Prophets. I did not come to destroy but to fulfill. For assuredly, I say to you, till heaven and earth pass away, one jot or one tittle will by no means pass from the law until all is fulfilled' " (Matthew 5:17, 18). After making this statement, Jesus amplified the spiritual significance of the sixth and seventh commandments. He also expanded and rejuvenated the spiritual purpose of the fourth commandment in the context of His several recorded Sabbath healings.

If, following His resurrection, Jesus had altered the day of rest and worship, He would have contradicted His own statement. Had the disciples and apostles changed the Sabbath to Sunday, they would have violated Jesus' statement as well. It goes without saying, then, that any alteration of the fourth commandment by any future leader must be viewed in the same light—as a deviation from the proclaimed Word of God and as a serious dereliction of responsibility to Jesus Christ Himself.

The missing link

With such evidence in mind, it is safe to say that generation after generation of Sunday advocates, however sincere and well meaning, have passed on a fictional narrative of the days following the Resurrection. This re-imagined story has taken on a life of its own, even though it has no basis in fact. It is an account that has propagated unwittingly to untold millions of people a serious misconception about first-century Christianity. Some would call this "revisionism"—the attempt to rewrite history according to one's own agenda.

Do either the book of Acts, which is the primary historical record of the first Christians, or other sources outside the Bible verify Dr. Kennedy's explanation? They do not. There is no clear biblical authorization or explanation for the abandonment of the seventh-day Sabbath. Neither is there even one description in the Bible of first century believers in Jesus abandoning the Sabbath in preference to Sunday sacredness.

Sunday-keeping Protestants are confronted with the mystery of the *missing link* in the transition from observance of the seventh day to the first day—when, God declared His commandments to be "perpetual" and standing "forever." It is this missing historical and biblical link that calls into question the longstanding perception of millions of people, both Christian and non-Christian, that Sunday is the "Lord's day."

Dr. Theodore Zahn, Lutheran historian and professor of theology at the University of Erlangen, wrote:

The Apostles could not have conceded to any other than one man the right to "change the customs Moses had given:" the Son of Man, who called Himself Lord also of the Sabbath day; but of Him they knew that He had neither transgressed nor abolished the Jewish Sabbath, but truly sanctified it. And they knew also, how He had threatened any of His disciples who might dare to abolish even one of the least of the commands of Moses.

But this has no one dared to do with the Sabbath commandment during the time of the Apostles. Certainly not with the territory of the Jewish Christendom; for they con-

tinued to keep the actual Sabbath. . . . Nor could any one have thought of such a thing within the Gentile Christian domain as far as Paul's influence reached. (*History of Sunday, Nobles of the Old Church*, P. T. Mallings, Christiania, 1879, pp. 33, 34; Norwegian, translated in Christian Edwardson, *Facts of Faith*, p. 86.)

Noted church historian Augustus Neander concurred:

The festival of Sunday, like all other festivals, was always only a human ordinance, and it was far from the intentions of the apostles to establish a Divine command in this respect, far from them, and from the early apostolic Church, to transfer the laws of the Sabbath to Sunday. . . . (Augustus Neander, *The History of the Christian Religion and Church*, Sanford and Swords, New York, 1843, Rose's translation, p. 186)

Again, we must ask of Sunday advocates: *Why must the seventh-day Sabbath be abandoned in order to honor the resurrection of Jesus, and why is there a complete absence of a Sunday theology in New Testament Scripture?*

On what basis can today's Christians continue to be instructed that Sunday observance began with the infant church of Jerusalem?

Where can it be shown that God withdrew the Creation blueprint of "blessedness" and sacredness of the seventh day?

If the seventh-day is no longer revered and sacred to God, when did Jesus relinquish His self-proclaimed title, "Lord of the Sabbath"?

What should one think and how should one feel if the Sabbath's sister institution from the Creation—marriage—were to be altered or abandoned in the era of the Christian church? Would one not be repulsed, and would one not think it worthwhile to come to its defense and preservation? Why then should the seventh-day Sabbath of the Creation be ignored, left behind, and abandoned by the very persons it was designed to bless (Mark 2:27)?

*I'd rather see heaven crash from the skies
than one grain of God's truth die.*
—Martin Luther

CHAPTER 9

Truth to Live and Die For

The issue of the change of God's worship day is vital to Christians everywhere. For nearly two millennia the Church has skirted the correction of this greatest of its faults, although many Christians have raised their voices to declare the ongoing validity of the Sabbath commandment. Some of these voices have been violently silenced and the records of their witness purposely destroyed.

The Bible urges believers to "contend earnestly for the faith once for all delivered to the saints" (Jude 3). If this biblical counsel had been followed faithfully in the early centuries of Christianity, many of the distortions of Christian teaching and non-biblical practices, including that of dismissing the seventh day, would not have occurred. Historian John Dowling described the rapid pace of the spiritual decline of the church in Rome:

> **There is scarcely anything which strikes the mind of the careful student of ancient ecclesiastical history with greater surprise than the comparatively early period at which many of the corruptions of Christianity, which are embodied in the Roman system, took their rise; yet it is not to be supposed that when the first originators of many of these unscriptural notions and practices planted those germs of corruption, they anticipated or even imagined that they would ever grow into such a vast and hideous system of superstition and error, as is that of Popery. (John Dowling,**

History of Romanism from the Earliest Corruptions of Christianity, 13th Edition, Edward Walker, New York, 1845, p. 65)

During the medieval centuries thousands of Christians would not join in the apostasy—the falling away from biblical teachings—forecast by the Apostle Paul (see 2 Thessalonians 2:3). These brave believers comprised the "wilderness church," which existed side by side with the medieval church.

Rome's missionaries, often supported by papal armies, extended the ranks of the medieval church by using Augustine's philosophy of "compel them to come in." Those who wished to remain faithful to the practices and teachings of the first-century church, which included observance of the sacred seventh day, retreated to isolated communities, "safe" cities and refuges in the mountain valleys of Spain, southern France, northern Italy, Moravia and Bohemia.

Few in modern times are aware of the heroic leaders of these believers. These included Vigilantius, Columbanus, Claude of Turin, Berengarius of France, Joannes Scotus Erigena, Peter de Bruys, Henry of Lausanne, Arnold of Brescia, and Peter Waldo—all of whom the leaders of the dominant church branded as heretics.[18]

At risk of their lives, tens of thousands united with these tireless leaders in various remote locations. Those who hunted and persecuted them gave them different names: Waldenses and Vallenses (people of the valleys), Insabbati or Insabbatati or Ensavates (observers of the Sabbath), Cathari (upholders of purity of life and doctrine), Leonists, Paulicians, Patarines, Berengarians, Petrobusians, Henricians, and Arnoldists (from their leader), Albigenses, Subalpini, and Passagians (from their region).

Comprised of merchants, artisans, royalty, scholars, university professors and students, farmers and tradesman—all were attracted by the beauty of Bible truth and by conviction born of love for Jesus. The motto of the wilderness church came from John 1:5: *Lux lucet in tenebris, which means* "Light Shining in the Darkness."

Living under extreme hardship, yet eager to advance their evangelical cause in spite of the danger, few lived out their natural lifespan. Many were subjected to exile, the inquisition, the dungeon, the rack or the stake. Unmentionable are the massacres and the entire villages and cities put to the sword.

While traces of the stories of their faithfulness survive, only the records of heaven contain the full story of this treacherous period in church history.

The question persists: *Why would those claiming the banner of the cross wish to extinguish by stealth, compromise, or apathy the Sabbath of which Jesus claimed to be LORD?*

The subtlety of substitution

Besides being subject to open hostility, God's gift of weekly rest for humanity has been challenged non-violently as well. From the era of Augustine, Pope Gregory I and Thomas Aquinas to the present, Sunday advocates have repeatedly attempted to dismiss the historic Sabbath day with fictional theologies under the pretense of exalting Christ. Unwittingly the inventors and proponents of these alternate theologies have played into the hands of the archenemy of Jesus, whose most devious strategy has been to replace Christ under the pretense of elevating Him.[19]

This subtle strategy of dismissing Christ by supplying a substitute that has the appearance of Christ has resulted in the summary abandonment of the divinely established Sabbath day. It has meant that the church substituted the humanly glorified Sunday for the Sabbath ostensibly to exalt and honor Christ in His resurrection. That's how believers can unwittingly violate the fourth commandment under the pretense of exalting and honoring Christ.

It would be facetious to ask if this strategy has been successful down through the centuries. Humans who depend on their own inclination are often mislead. Even today, millions of God-fearing, humble-hearted believers are bound intellectually and emotionally to this strategy of substitution. Unknowingly, they are victims of this age-old spiritual deception.

Why this issue matters

Regardless of these detractors of the Sabbath through the centuries, the Bible record of God's expressed will has not changed. The sacred fourth commandment still stands as the unbending "gold standard" for every generation.

The Apostle Paul urged the importance of God's law for believers as he defined sin: "**. . . by the law is the knowledge of sin**" (Romans 3:20). "**. . . I would not have known sin except through the law. . . For I would not have known covetousness unless the law had said, 'You shall not covet'**" (Romans 7:7). "**The wages of sin is death. . . .**" (Romans 6:23).

Theologian R. C. Sproul gives this sobering definition of sin:

When God issues a law, when He legislates a kind of behavior, it is our duty as His creatures to do as He says. A moral obligation to conform to that law is imposed on us justly from His hand. When we don't conform, we are breaking that law, which means we are committing a crime in the sight of God. . . (*The Truth of the Cross*, Reformation Trust Publishers, Lake Mary, Florida, 2007, p. 40)

According to this definition, is it not fair to say that a collective, generational crime has been perpetrated against the Creator God?

And what of those who would dare to tamper with the Divine Code? In doing so, have not masses of God-fearing people been defrauded and deceived into dereliction of duty as presented in the Word of God? If there is no divine mandate for Sunday sacredness or for the dismantling of the seventh-day Sabbath of the fourth commandment, then worldwide Christianity, however sincere, is facing a monumental moral dilemma with the Sovereign of the universe.

In the abandonment of the Sabbath of Creation, is it not evident that the greater portion of Protestant and Catholic Christianity is unwittingly out of step with the very One who is rightly acclaimed as the cornerstone of the Christian faith and who declared Himself "LORD even of the Sabbath"?

The ultimate question
Many say their worship on Sunday is not a matter of conscience, but of convenience in meeting when other Christians gather for wor-

ship. The ultimate question remains: *Will our relationship with Jesus be based upon expediency and human convenience or upon the wisdom and expressed will of our Redeemer? Will we continue to observe a worship day that is of human origin or will we choose the sacred time that is of the Creator's design? Will we follow the authoritative voice of the Lawgiver Himself—Jesus Christ—or will we give ear to the merely human ecclesiastical mandate?*

Now that you have learned about this ever-present dilemma, someone is sure to press you to abandon further study, insisting that this issue over the fourth commandment doesn't matter anymore—that it isn't really that important. Others will attempt to paint the issue of the Sabbath as legalistic, even though they would never claim that Jesus' consistent Sabbath observance was legalistic, nor that the fourth commandment He gave is itself legalistic, nor that the observance of the Sabbath by our first parents in Eden after the Creation was legalistic. Yet, count on it—someone will urge you to put this Bible issue out of your mind.

Do those who are in love with God and His Son, Jesus Christ, consider God's commands—even specific ones—to be unreasonable or burdensome (1 John 5:1–3)? And do those who are in love with God work hard at devising explanations so they can disregard God's requirements?

Consider the frame of mind of the One who went to the cross:

When you lift up the Son of Man, then you will know that I am He, and that I do nothing of Myself; but as My Father taught Me, I speak these things. And He who sent Me is with Me. The father has not left Me alone, for *I always do those things that please Him.* (John 8:28, 29; emphasis supplied)

Our LORD has given us a gallant and honorable example.

Those from among you shall build the old waste places. . .
And you shall be called the Repairer of the Breach,
the Restorer of Streets to Dwell in. —The LORD God (Isaiah 58:12)

CHAPTER 10
Restoring the Original LORD's Day

As we have seen, the seventh day of Creation week is the handiwork of God Himself. It is Jesus who said that He was LORD of it; it was He who spoke it into existence. It stands to reason that, if Jesus made no claim to reverse this command, human attempts to dismiss the Sabbath's sacredness are in actuality a dismantling of the handiwork of the LORD Jesus Christ. Thus, something vital has faded from view. Through the centuries, a biblical treasure has gone missing, the Christian message has been weakened because of it and all humanity is less than it was meant to be.

University professor and scholar Sigve Tonstad declared:

God is the primary subject of the seventh day. When we speak of the lost meaning of the seventh day, therefore, we are speaking of meaning that has been lost concerning God.[20]

Will this lost meaning concerning God continue to prevail in the twenty-first century? Will modern Christianity be shortchanged of its most ancient divine blessing and of its most potent exhibit against macro evolution?

Dr. Tonstad made this prediction: "To the extent that it [the seventh day] is part of God's story, it cannot be suppressed indefinitely. It must reassert itself to complete its God-ordained mission; it cannot remain in permanent exile."[21]

So, now we turn our attention to the meaning of the seventh day and the story of its resurgence into worldwide prominence once again.

The Sabbath migrates to America

The seeds of the Creation Sabbath arrived early in the history of the America, brought by immigrants from the European countries. Many came seeking freedom of conscience and expression. However, the significance of the seventh day began to reach a wider public audience in the mid-nineteenth century when a prominent, retired New England sea captain named Joseph Bates was given an article promoting the biblical reasons for the sacredness of the seventh day and its consecration during Creation week.

Years before, while he was at sea, Bates had begun to read a Bible that his Christian wife Prudence had placed in his luggage. With his worldview dramatically changed by it and having earned a small fortune for that time, Bates retired from the sea in his thirties to invest himself in advancing the gospel under conviction regarding the soon return of Jesus Christ in all His glory. However, when he and his Bible-believing friends discovered the seventh-day Sabbath of Scripture, his passion for its significance, as he saw it relating to final events on earth, moved him with urgency to advance the meaning of the lost seventh day. His biblical apologetic *The Seventh Day Sabbath—A Perpetual Sign,* published in 1846, became a compelling read.

The enthusiasm and passion with which Bates and his associates carried out their mission was a result of their study of the prophecies of the book of Revelation. Chapter 14 predicts that the gospel message will circle the globe before Christ's return. John the Revelator wrote: "And I saw another angel flying in the midst of heaven, having the everlasting gospel to preach to those who dwell on earth—to every nation, tribe, tongue, and people" (Revelation 14:6). According to this prediction, Christ's return will have an advanced announcement and worldwide expectation.

Bates noticed that this gospel message of the grace of God was to be given within the setting of a call to respect and honor God, that God's time of judgment has come, accompanied by an urgent appeal for the whole human family to turn in worship to the Creator God—

. . . saying with a loud voice, "Fear God and give glory to Him, for the hour of His judgment has come; and worship Him who made heaven and earth, the sea and springs of water." (Revelation 14:7)

It must be noted with some significance that, at the same time that renewed attention would be given to the worship of the Creator God, the writings of Charles Darwin would launch an opposing worldview of evolutionistic science with a resulting rise in secularism, naturalism and atheistic culture.

Bates saw Revelation 14:6, 7 as a heaven-ordained warning happening simultaneously with the "time of the end." He also associated a renewed worldwide call to observance of the Creation Sabbath as the direct fulfillment of Revelation's imperative to " 'worship Him who made heaven and earth, the sea, and springs of water.' " After all, he reasoned, here were words taken directly from the fourth commandment itself—" '. . . the LORD *made the heavens and the earth, the sea, and* all that is in them . . .' " (Exodus 20:11, emphasis supplied to mark the words in Revelation 14:7).

A present and accelerating world-wide movement

What has happened regarding the Creation Sabbath during the intervening years from the 1850s to the present?

It can be said that today, in a single denomination alone, over thirty million followers of Jesus Christ in nearly every country of the world observe the seventh-day Sabbath. On the African continent, there are over five million Sabbath-observing Christians. In Central and South America, over seven million people observe the sacred time of the Creation Sabbath. In the city of Sao Paulo, Brazil, alone, there are 300 Sabbath-observing congregations. Ten percent of the population on the island of Jamaica are Sabbath-observing Christians, and this includes the chief governing magistrate of the island. In North America, over one million Sabbath-observers weekly assemble to worship Jesus in over 6000 church locations.

Notable prominent Sabbath-observing figures in America are Barry Black who is Chaplain of the U.S. Senate; pioneering neurosurgeon Dr. Ben Carson of Johns Hopkins University Hospital in Baltimore, Maryland; Wintley Phipps, vocal gospel recording artist and soloist for two presidential inauguration ceremonies and founder of the U.S. Dream Academy; and gospel vocal recording artists Steve Green and Michael Card.

A more personal story to me is that of Fredrick and Johanne. In 1910 this couple met on a German cargo-passenger ship destined for New York harbor. Fredrick had been sailing the seven seas as a German merchant marine. Johanne was a German immigrant coming to America. Upon entry at port, Fredrick jumped ship and soon married Johanne. They eventually made their home in the American Northwest and started a family.

Years had passed when tragedy occurred. As their oldest son William was attempting to cross an intersection, he was struck down by a Model T Ford—with a fatal blow to the head. Six-year old Emil, William's little brother (and my father-to-be), was an eyewitness. Following the loss, Johanne entered an extended period of mourning, which led her to draw upon her Lutheran faith and a renewed interest in the Word of God. As providence would have it, she and my grandfather would not only find that the Bible's answer to death was in the coming resurrection at the return of Jesus, but they also discovered the meaning of the sacred time of the seventh day. These are my personal roots to the story of Christianity's lost world-class treasure.

So the question persists—*How have these millions across the globe come to Bible convictions about the authenticity of the original "*Lord's *day"? And why would increasing numbers of Bible-loving, grace-filled believers from varied ethnic and social backgrounds be re-examining and returning to the Creator God's time of sacred rest? Are the Scripture evidences compelling enough?*

This is the pursuit of our next chapter—*The Ten Top Evidences for the Creation Sabbath.* Yet, before we begin, let this be an introductory thought to set the stage . . .

Many readers may be surprised to think of the Bible's patriarchs from Adam to Enoch, from Methuselah and Noah to Abraham, as seventh-day observers. Though most know that the prophets and writers of the Old Testament and all the apostles and authors of the New Testament were Sabbath-observers. More important than who kept the Sabbath is the fact that the central figure of the Bible and the author of Revelation, Jesus Christ (Revelation 1:1), who epitomizes the grace of God to the human family, took the self-proclaimed title—"LORD even of the Sabbath." It is this awareness of "sacred time" that Bible students must bring to their study of the Scriptures.

It is on this basis that the angelic message of Revelation 14 is brought to the world's attention at the very time of the end—**"worship Him who made heaven and the earth, the sea and springs of water."** As a student of Bible prophecy, are you left wondering what this means and how relevant and urgent the subject of sacred time is?

The plans of he LORD stand firm forever,
the purposes of his heart through all generations.
—King David (Psalm 33:11, NIV)

CHAPTER 11
The Top Ten Evidences for the Creation Sabbath

EVIDENCE #1. The Sabbath originated at the Creation.

Jesus expressed confidence in the seven-day Creation account of Genesis, chapters 1 and 2, when He answered His questioners by saying, " 'Have you not read that He who made them in the beginning made them male and female . . .' " (Matthew 19:4, 5).

Jesus' self-chosen title, " 'LORD even of the Sabbath' " (Matthew 12:8), identifies Him as the Sabbath's Maker. Thus, He claimed rightful ownership of the Sabbath, and in so doing, declared His divinity and creative power in Creation week.

In announcing that " 'the Sabbath was made for man [Greek, *anthropos*]. . .' " (Mark 2:27), Jesus spoke of sacred time—the seventh day—as an integral component of the blueprint for humanity at Creation. It is part of the original relational "DNA" for all humans. Along with marriage, it was designed for humanity in Creation's perfection before the entrance of sin (Genesis 2:1–3). God is a God of people, and the seventh-day Sabbath is the divine centerpiece of His devotion to the human family. As such it renders itself a prime target for disruption and distortion by God's enemy.

The weekly cycle of seven 24-hour days is God's idea. This measure of time, in an unbroken cycle from Creation week, is common to almost all nations.* The weekly cycle and the Sabbath day are among the best evidences validating the historicity of the Creation story of

---

* Knowledge of this seven-day cycle before Moses is reflected in the predominance of seven days as a period of time in Genesis 7:4, 10; 8:10, 12, 14; 31:23; 50:10; Exodus 7:25; 12:15, and in the use of "week" to describe a period of time in Genesis 29:27, 28.

Genesis and humanity's origin. King David assures us that Creation week was not an elongated period of time: "Let all the inhabitants of the world stand in awe of Him. For he spoke, and it came to be; he commanded, and it stood firm" (Psalm 33:8, 9, ESV).

There are those who question the Sabbath being kept through the centuries beginning with Creation week. Yet, most of these same ones do not question that marriage, the Sabbath's sister institution, was practiced from Creation onward. Jesus identifies for whom the Sabbath was made: " 'the Sabbath was made for man [all humanity including those between Creation week and the giving of the Law at Mt. Sinai] . . .' " (Mark 2:28). The recent contention that the Sabbath originated at Sinai instead of at Creation does not stand on firm historical footing. Martin Luther himself commented on the pre-Sinai Sabbath test recorded in Exodus 16:4, 22–30: "Hence, you can see that the Sabbath was before the Law of Moses came, and has existed from the beginning of the world. Especially have the devout, who have preserved the true faith, met together and called upon God on this day."[22] It stands to reason that, if the sacred time of the Sabbath is designed for humans to be in relationship with their Creator, it would begin at their creation. As it was "blessed" and "sanctified" (set apart distinctly for divine interaction), it was set in motion, becoming effective immediately.

Many noteworthy spokesmen have validated the Sabbath's longevity. In debating Martin Luther, Eck declared: "If you. . . turn from the church to the Scriptures alone, then you must keep the Sabbath with the Jews, *which has been kept from the beginning of the world.*" (emphasis supplied)

Martin Luther did not question the Sabbath's early origin, describing its purpose in his commentary on Genesis 1, 2:

God blessed the Sabbath and sanctified it to himself. It is moreover to be remarked that God did this to no other creature. God did not sanctify to himself the heaven nor the earth nor any other creature. But God did sanctify to himself the seventh day. This was especially designed of God, to cause us to understand that the "seventh day" is to be especially devoted to divine worship. . . It follows therefore

from this passage, that if Adam had stood in his innocence and had not fallen he would yet have observed the "seventh day" as sanctified, holy and sacred. . . Nay, even after the fall he held the "seventh day" sacred; that is, he taught on that day his own family. This is testified by the offerings made by his two sons, Cain and Abel. The Sabbath therefore has, from the beginning of the world, been set apart for the worship of God. . . For all these things are implied and signified in the expression "sanctified." (Martin Luther, *Commentary on Genesis*, edited by J. N. Lenker, vol. 1, Lutherans in All Lands Co., Minneapolis, Minnesota, 1904, pp. 138–140)

First century Jewish author, Philo of Alexandria, considered the Sabbath as having been made for all humanity:

But after the whole world had been completed according to the perfect nature of the number six, the Father hallowed the day following, the seventh, praising it, and calling it holy. For that day is the festival, not of any one city or one country, but of all the earth; a day which alone it is right to call the day of festival for all people, and the birthday of the world. (Philo of Alexandria, "On the Creation," Section XXX (89), in *The Works of Philo: Complete and Unabridged*, Hendrickson, Peabody, Massachusetts, 1996, p. 13)

The first century Jewish historian Josephus cited God's rest at the Creation as the reason for observance of the Sabbath:

Moses says, That in just six days the world and all that is therein was made; and that the seventh day was a rest and a release from the labor of such operations;—whence it is that we celebrate a rest from our labors on that day, and call it the Sabbath; which word denotes rest in the Hebrew tongue. (Flavius Josephus, "Antiquities of the Jews," book 1, chapter 1, section 1, in *The Works of Josephus: Complete and Unabridged,* Hendrickson, Peabody, Massachusetts,1996, p. 29)

Professor and author Sigve Tonstad explained that in blessing and consecrating the seventh day, God has made "a permanent imprint on human time."[23] The Creator has chosen to be intimately involved with His creation and the Sabbath is His promise to the human family "conveying the message of God's enduring and faithful participation in human reality."

"The Sabbath cannot be destroyed unless God forgets it," Professor Tonstad added. "Only the One who instituted the Sabbath can rescind its sanctity."[24]

With this understanding, human attempts to dispel the Sabbath day can be seen as fallacious and even nonsensical. The Sabbath as a historical event has been indelibly tied to the point of origin of the human race. To alter or dispense with the weekly Creation Sabbath is to devalue the Creation story itself and to rob the Creator of His continuing ultimate goal for the weekly Sabbath—to bring the human family into intimate relationship with Himself.

Thus, regardless of human indifference, the Sabbath continues. Swiss author C. A. Keller wrote:

Just as the rainbow automatically appears, so the Sabbath comes back regularly without human contribution. The Sabbath is itself holy time regardless of whether man keeps it because God has sanctified this day for all time. The remaining question for the people is only whether to recognize this holiness and relate themselves to it in their sphere.[25]

Jewish author Pinchas Peli agreed, writing, "It remains up to us to let her in, to receive her properly . . ."[26]

The ultimate question for Creation week is to answer why people need the seventh-day weekly Sabbath. The reality of Creation that humans are made in the "image of God" is a prime reason (Genesis 1:26, 27).

Old Testament professor at the Andrews University Theological Seminary, Jiri Moskala, explained that the Creation week is God-centered and not man-centered. Just as the six days of Creation are climaxed in the seventh day, human completion culminates as people are placed in relationship with the One in whose "image" they were made.

Humans are entirely dependent upon God, and they experience completeness in intimate relationship with Him. Being made in His "image," humans may choose to be a reflection of their Maker in character, disposition and wisdom and thereby be a credit to His renown and glory throughout the galaxies. So humans are called to imitate their Creator. Since God rested on the seventh day (Genesis 2:1–3), humans likewise, in imitation of their Maker, rest on the seventh day in the recurring weekly cycle.

The twenty-first century modern is in acute need of the Sabbath pause. World economies and governments are fiercely interconnected. Competition, the desire for excellence, prestige and status drive the workplace and wear on body and mind.

In her article *The Dangerous Wager of Success,* author Jen Pollock Michel urged: ". . . Sabbath has always been a transaction of trust. When we pause, we create necessary and holy distance from the petulant idea that we are ultimately in charge of anything. When we rest, we remember our limited role as creatures. Sabbath is the habit of humility we can wear every week, forcing us to relinquish illusions of our indispensability. In humble worship, and rest, we finally learn to remember that we are productive only as God establishes the work of our hands (Psalm 90:17)" (*Christianity Today*, July/August 2013, p. 78).

The twenty-first century has witnessed an exaggerated spirit of independence and secularization, resulting in a loss of the sense of the sacred. Professor Jiri Maskala illustrated how the Sabbath experience challenges self-sufficiency in the human spirit:

God made a special provision so that humans may stay truly human and humane: He created the Sabbath and set it apart as a special and irreplaceable gift for the first couple and for all following generations so they might stay in right relationship with Him and thus live honestly and nobly. . . If humans will live in dependence on God, everything will be all right. Should they start to act autonomously, they will become tyrants. They will lose the sense of sacredness,

then nothing will be sacred to them—they will think they can do anything. Sabbath therefore is a safeguard for humanity and a wall against idolatry. (Dr. Jiri Moskala, "The Sabbath in the First Creation Account," *Perspective Digest,* vol. 12, no. 2 [Spring 2007], p. 48)

That this is so can be seen in what has become of the angel Lucifer and the angelic beings who chose to disconnect with him from their Maker. This dysfunction is repeated in the lives of those who choose to live without reference to the One who made them.

Humans by nature will always be dependent upon God as their life source (Acts 17:28). This is why the seventh-day "rest" has the status of a moral obligation to God. As a bird is dependent on its wings to sustain flight, so humans need God to sustain their happiness and well-being. It is for this reason that the Creator, like a protective lover, has declared the seventh-day as valid for all time—even for eternity:

"For as the new heavens and the new earth which I will make shall remain before Me," says the LORD, "so shall your descendants and your name remain. And it shall come to pass that from one New Moon to another [the endless cycle of time], and from one Sabbath to another, all flesh [saved humanity, that is—both Jew and Gentile] shall come to worship before Me," says the LORD. (Isaiah 66:22, 23)

Considering all of the above, it is difficult to imagine that the fourth commandment Sabbath would be thought of by some as a later addition and therefore be classified as ceremonial, temporary and exclusively Jewish.

EVIDENCE #2. Jesus made and lived the Sabbath.

The Old Testament gospel prophet Isaiah made the following prediction about the Messiah that would be fulfilled by Jesus:

The LORD is well pleased for His righteousness sake; He will magnify the law and make it honorable. (Isaiah 42:21)

74

None other than Jesus, the Christ—the benchmark of all truth—rightly proclaimed Himself as "LORD even of the Sabbath" (Matthew 12:8). As LORD, Jesus is governor of the Sabbath and defines what it is and how He meant for it to benefit humanity.

Does it appear, from the writers of the Gospels, that Jesus treated the Sabbath as if it were exclusively "Jewish" and, therefore, ceremonial and temporary? Do the Gospel writings give any indication that He was preparing for the Sabbath to fade away following His mission to earth? Indeed, what does the record show?

As the only righteous, sinless One, Jesus came in His humanity to perfectly live out the law that He Himself had spoken in thunder tones from Mt. Sinai (1 Corinthians 10:1–4). The Ten Commandment law was at that time inscribed by the finger of God in two tables of stone; but when Jesus came, they were presented in living, human form—that is, in the person of Jesus Christ. As predicted, Jesus came to magnify the law (including the fourth commandment) and make it "honorable" (Isaiah 42:21).

Jesus lived out the real meaning of the Ten Commandments, which, in Scripture, are repeatedly associated with righteousness (Isaiah 51:7; Psalm 119:172; Romans 8:4). Jesus is the Righteous One—He is the law on display in human interaction with real people. He made righteousness attractive and desirable.

The Apostle Paul assures us that "Jesus Christ is the same yesterday, today, and forever" (Hebrews 13:8). It stands to reason, then, that, since Jesus is the law personified, we can be assured that His life's description of righteousness (the Ten Commandments) is also the same "yesterday, today, and forever" —including the fourth commandment Sabbath.

It is for these reasons, as well as because of the numerous Sabbath healing narratives found in the Gospels, that Jesus Christ is the Bible's and the world's greatest authoritative proponent of the seventh-day Creation Sabbath.

Because the Creation Sabbath is deeply relational—a restful, undistracted meeting place in time between the human family and their Maker—Jesus cared deeply to secure its success. Following the anointing of the Holy Spirit at His baptism and the grueling wilderness temptations, Jesus chose the Sabbath as the day on which to publicly inaugurate His ministry and mission. It happened in His home town, Nazareth (Luke 4:16–30). Quoting prophecy, Jesus briefly set the tone and objective of his ministry:

The Spirit of the Lord is upon Me, because He has anointed Me to preach the gospel to the poor. He has sent Me to heal the brokenhearted, to preach deliverance to the captives and recovery of sight to the blind, to set at liberty those who are oppressed, to preach the acceptable year of the Lord. (Luke 4:18, 19; quoting from Isaiah 61:1, 2)

Jesus' personal practice ("custom," Luke 4:16) of Sabbath observance included teaching, healing, fellowship and both individual and corporate worship. It was normal on the seventh day to find Jesus at the temple or in a synagogue teaching, confronting disease, or meeting people with their burdens, needs and questions.

With decades of abuse from scores of nonsensical restrictions devised by the Jewish sects, the Sabbath day needed urgent reformation. Christ's several intentional, daring confrontations of religious leaders over these Sabbath abuses were the avenue by which He liberated sacred time from the traditions of human invention, which had become "hoary with age." The numerous Sabbath healings Jesus performed cast a spiritually celebrant ring to the Sabbath and demonstrated its real meaning—spiritual refreshment, physical rest and restoration, and recovery from the bondage of sin. Jesus' joyous, liberating precepts and practice, focusing on communion with God, were in great contrast to the burdensome Sabbath traditions of human invention.

In this way, Jesus magnified the fourth commandment and set it in its rightful place—honoring the Lord God the Creator and centering the heart and mind on God's love, mercy, and righteousness. In reality Jesus is the reason for the Sabbath—His presence is the cause of its sacredness, and He is the Author of the human race for whom the Sabbath was made.

As previously noted, the Sabbath, as revived by Jesus, was carried on into the Christian church era. Every gospel writer in the New Testament (writing to both Jews and Gentiles decades after the Resurrection) openly records these Sabbath reforms initiated by Jesus in order that coming generations of believers would ever enjoy the true blessings intended by Him through the seventh-day Sabbath.

Did Jesus live and reform the Sabbath just to have it later discarded? When speaking of His relationship with the heavenly Father, Jesus said: " '. . . I do nothing of myself; but as My Father taught Me, I speak these things. . . . I always do those things that please Him. . .' " (John 8:28, 29). Remembering God's holy day does please Him.

The Sabbath in the New Covenant

Jesus is the Author and primary focus of the New Covenant experience for every believer. He is our King, our High Priest, our Sin-bearer and the Mediator between God and human beings. It is through His sacrifice on the cross and His shed blood that our sins are forgiven. It is in Him that the believer becomes a new creation (2 Corinthians 5:17).

At the sacrificial shedding of Jesus' blood on the cross, the Old Covenant ceremonial laws of the sanctuary foreshadowing the Messiah became obsolete because their symbolism had become reality. Moreover, the righteous Ten Commandment law placed inside the ark of the covenant, which describes the righteousness of Jesus for the Old Testament, is now lived out perfectly in the New Testament in the person of Jesus Christ.

What was always God's purpose now has its best opportunity to be implanted by the Holy Spirit in the New Covenant "Israel of God" (Galatians 6:16). Here is the heart of the New Covenant promise:

> **For this is the covenant that I will make with the house of Israel: After those days, says the Lord, I will put My laws in their minds and write them on their hearts; and I will be their God, and they shall be My people. . . . all shall know Me from the least of them to the greatest of them. For I will be merciful to their unrighteousness, and their sins and their lawless deeds I will remember no more.** (Hebrews 8:10–12; fulfillment of Jeremiah 31:31– 34)

When sinners see that Jesus paid in full their debt of sin on the cross, a new motivation grips the soul—love. A new allegiance to the righteous Christ is born—a desire to walk as Jesus walked (1 John 2:6). A new, fresh attitude to the law of God is embraced. It is intellectually appreciated and emotionally internalized—in the mind and heart. The disciple John described New Covenant love:

By this we know that we love the children of God, when we love God and keep His commandments. For this is the love of God, that we keep His commandments. And His commandments are not burdensome. (1 John 5:1–3)

The righteousness of God's commandments, which includes the fourth commandment of the seventh-day Sabbath, is the life legacy that the crucified Savior took to the cross with Him. His death and resurrection forever sealed it as the standard of righteousness in the New Covenant. The righteousness seen in the life of Jesus Christ is the same before and after the cross. The righteous requirement of the seventh-day sacred time is the same for humans in every age.

Here is Paul's powerful explanation of the good news of God's grace:

For what the law could not do in that it was weak through the flesh, God did by sending His own Son in the likeness of sinful flesh, on account of sin: He condemned sin in the flesh, that the righteousness of the law might be fulfilled in us who do not walk according to the flesh but according to the Spirit. (Romans 8:3, 4)

The book of Hebrews calls the New Covenant the "everlasting covenant" (Hebrews 13:20). It was first introduced to Adam and Eve (Genesis 3:15), then confirmed with Abraham (Romans 4) and finally ratified and secured by Jesus Christ (Matthew 26:26–29; Galatians 3:26–29).

Surprisingly, the Old Testament (and pre-Sinai) patriarch Abraham is the New Testament's prime example of the New Covenant experience. In Romans, Paul described the fundamental application to all who believe:

But now the righteousness of God apart from the law is revealed, being witnessed by the Law and the Prophets, even the righteousness of God which is through faith in Jesus Christ to all and on all who believe. . . . For what does the Scripture say? "Abraham believed God, and it was accounted to [imputed or credited to] him for righteousness." (Romans 3:21, 22; 4:3)

The Covenant that God made with Abraham and his descendants is called in Genesis the "everlasting covenant" (Genesis 17:7). In the New Testament it is offered to all who have "put on Christ" (Galatians 3:26–29).

Regarding the relationship of the law with the New Covenant experience, Paul asked an important question: "Do we then make void the law through faith?" And what was Paul's answer? "Certainly not! On the contrary, we establish the law" (Romans 3:31).

Does the New Covenant contain a new law? Dr. Samuele Bacchiocchi explains:

. . . the New Covenant . . . consists not in the replacement of the Ten Commandments with simpler and better laws, but in the *internalization* of God's Law. . . . [Jeremiah 31:33] teaches us that the difference between the Old and New Covenants is not a difference between "Law" and "love." Rather, it is a difference between failure to internalize God's Law, which results in disobedience, and successful internalization of God's Law, which results in loving obedience. (*The Sabbath Under Crossfire,* Biblical Perspectives, Berrien Springs, Michigan, 1998, p. 113)

In other words, it is through the enabling power of the Holy Spirit that the New Covenant believer is able to internalize God's law.

Does Abraham's pre-Sinai experience of being credited with the righteousness of God by faith show that God's laws had been written in his mind and heart, as is stated in the New Covenant (Hebrews 8:10–12)? God Himself provided this witness:

79

". . . in your seed all the nations of the earth shall be blessed; because Abraham obeyed My voice and kept My charge, My commandments, My statutes, and My laws." (Genesis 26:4, 5)

We should hasten to affirm that Abraham's obedience was not motivated to earn merit with God, but was from respect and gratitude to his Provider.

It is now possible for those who profess to have "put on Christ" to examine whether their New Covenant experience parallels that of Abraham whose neighbors considered him a "mighty prince" (Genesis 23:6) and who is described in Scripture as "the friend of God" (James 2:23).

EVIDENCE **#3**. The Sabbath is a moral issue.

Is the seventh day in the twenty-first century still "blessed" and sacred as it was at Creation and during the life of Jesus? Does God still see it as morally binding on all humanity? Does the title "LORD of the Sabbath" still rank as valid in describing Jesus?

The Bible answer to all of these questions is *Yes!*—and good reason will be shown in this section. However strange as it may seem, some Christian leaders over the course of time would answer *No.*

A common oversight made by some Bible students is to make no distinction between the weekly Creation Sabbath of the fourth commandment and the annual (once a year) ceremonial sabbaths that are attached to the sanctuary sacrificial system.

The weekly Sabbath predates the annual sabbaths by over two millennia. In Scripture, when God distinguishes between the two, He refers to the weekly Creation Sabbath as "My Sabbath" (Exodus 31:13; Ezekiel 20:12), "holy to the LORD" (Exodus 31:15) and "the sabbaths of the LORD" (Leviticus 23:37, 38). For the annual ceremonial sabbaths, He uses the term "your sabbaths" (Leviticus 23:32) or "a sabbath" (Leviticus 16:31).

The feast sabbaths may occur on any day of the week, much like Independence Day, New Year's Day and Christmas, while the weekly Sabbath is *always* on the seventh day of the week.

The weekly Sabbath is often spoken of as the "sign" that distinguishes God's relationship with His people as they are being "sanctified" by Him (Exodus 31:13; Ezekiel 20:12). The yearly sabbaths are several "feasts" at which sacrifices were offered (Exodus 23:14–17). When Jesus was twelve years old, His parents took Him to the "feast of the Passover" in Jerusalem (Luke 2:41, 42).

The annual feasts prefigured events in the plan of salvation that were to take place in the future. On the other hand, the weekly Sabbath looked back to humankind's noble origin in Creation as God's masterful design. Every week the Sabbath brought Israel to worship and reverence Him and to remember their complete dependence on Him.

Below is a succinct, recent statement from a seminary professor, passing as an explanation for the dissolution of the weekly Creation Sabbath:

We believe the Old Testament regulations governing Sabbath observance are ceremonial, not moral, aspects of the law. As such, they are no longer in force, but have passed away along with the sacrificial system, the Levitical priesthood, and all other aspects of Moses' law that prefigured Christ.

This statement may be true for the ceremonial "regulations" for sacrifice on the Sabbath, but it is not true for the Sabbath itself. Apparently, the author of the statement fails to recognize (1) the distinction between moral law, defined by the Ten Commandments, and ceremonial law prefiguring the coming Messiah; (2) the fourth commandment points back to the Creation event rather than forward to a future fulfillment, which is necessary for a ceremonial regulation; (3) the seventh-day Sabbath was considered morally binding by the Jews, by Jesus Himself, and by early Jewish and Gentile Christians.

The one who made this statement is a current well-known Christian radio teacher who is also the president of a theological seminary.[27] His statement, and others like it, maintains that the Sabbath of the fourth commandment, since the cross, is no longer a "day" in time but, rather, a continuous experience of "resting" in Christ. Therefore, in this way of thinking, it is justified to select another "day" to honor Jesus or to have no particular "day" at all.

This viewpoint is not a new rationale for the abandonment of the Creation Sabbath; it is an echo from the past.

We respond by asking: *What are the biblical evidences for the perpetuity of the weekly Sabbath? What distinguishes the historic seventh-day Sabbath as a moral issue and separates it from the annual ceremonial sabbaths?* Let readers judge for themselves:

Exhibit A: The Lord Himself declared that the Sabbath was "perpetual" (valid for all time) and "eternal."

Before Moses descended from Mt. Sinai with the two tables of stone written on by God (Exodus 31:18; 32:15, 16), the Lord stipulated a Sabbath agreement with Israel—the nation that would be the guardians of the Ten Commandments, living them out and giving them to the whole world. These are the Lord's exact words:

> **Therefore the children of Israel shall keep the Sabbath, to observe the Sabbath throughout their generations as a *perpetual* [valid for all time] covenant. It is a sign between Me and the children of Israel *forever*; for in six days the Lord made the heavens and the earth, and on the seventh day He rested and was refreshed.** (Exodus 31:16, 17, emphasis supplied)

When God had completed delivering the terms of the agreement, He gave Moses the two tables of stone—the Ten Commandments, the moral code for the whole world. Of these commandments, God singled out the fourth for special recognition. It is these same commandments that God proposed to place in the mind and heart of His people—the Israel of God (Galatians 6:16)—in the New Covenant (Hebrews 8:10; 10:16; Jeremiah 31:31–33). (Other things that God called "perpetual" were limited by the existence of the priesthood and the earthly sanctuary/tabernacle. See Exodus 29:9; 30:8; Leviticus 3:17; 6:20; 24:9.)

Reality cannot be changed. That a person's birth date is a certain day, cannot be altered. In the same way, Creation is history, and,

82

therefore, the seventh-day of the week is the memorial of the LORD's historic creative event. The seventh day is "sacred time," honoring the Creator—it is a "permanent imprint in time."

Exhibit B: The Sabbath is written in tables that were kept separate from other regulations.

God next instructed Moses to place the tables of stone (also known as the "testimony") into the Ark of the Covenant, which resided in the Most Holy Place of the LORD's Sanctuary (Deuteronomy 10:1–5). Above the tables of stone rested the covering of the "mercy seat" over which two cherubim spread their wings. It was from above the mercy seat and between the two cherubim that God would speak to Moses (Exodus 25:20–25).

The Ten Commandments (including the fourth) are the standard of God's righteousness. They are the standard by which all humans will be judged (James 2:11, 12). This is what makes it God's moral law—and the fourth commandment is part of it.

After a time, Moses completed his writing in a book of the civil, ceremonial and health instructions that God had given him while they were on Mt. Sinai (referred to as the "statues and judgments and laws," Leviticus 26:46). This book contained the regulations and sacrifices related to the sanctuary services, the rules that governed the Levite priests, and the outline of feast day annual sabbaths that were a part of the Feast of Unleavened Bread, the Feast of Weeks (Pentecost), Trumpets, the Day of Atonement, and the Feast of Tabernacles (Leviticus 23:7, 8, 11, 21, 24, 25, 32, 35, 36, 39).

When this "book of the law" was completed, God instructed Moses to place the book *beside* the Ark of the Covenant (Deuteronomy 31:24–26), while the Ten Commandments, written by God Himself, were placed *within* the Ark (Exodus 25:21).

The Sabbath of the Ten Commandment moral law stands apart from the sabbaths in the book of the law in which were listed the ceremonial, annual feast sabbaths. The first is "eternal;" God wrote it in stone; the second is "temporary;" God had Moses write it in a book. The first is moral, an expression of God's righteous character; the second is made up of ceremonial symbols, prefiguring the plan of salvation and the Messiah to come.

Exhibit C: The Sabbath law is to be written in the heart.

There are four manifestations of the moral law. First, God spoke the Ten Commandments audibly from Mt. Sinai to the two million Israelites. This means that Israel heard the voice of their Maker speak the fourth commandment along with the other nine (Exodus 20).

Second, God wrote the Ten Commandments in stone. This implies permanent, universal status. Moses was instructed to place the stone tablets inside the Ark of the Covenant where they would be guarded by angels (Exodus 31:18; Deuteronomy 5:22; 9:10).

Third, Jesus the Messiah fulfilled the prediction of Isaiah that the Ten Commandment law would be magnified and made honorable (Isaiah 42:21). Jesus reformed the Sabbath and proclaimed Himself the LORD of the Sabbath (Matthew 12:8). The righteous life of Jesus is the law expressed in human form, a living illustration of righteousness. The person of Jesus is the supreme expression of the Law of God.

Fourth, God Himself promised in the New Covenant: "I will put my law in their minds, and write it on their hearts; and I will be their God, and they shall be My people" (Jeremiah 31:33; specified as "laws" in Hebrews 8:10; 10:16). The righteous life of Jesus would be fulfilled in the lives of His followers, who, through the Holy Spirit, have "put on Christ" (Galatians 3:27). The Apostle John assures us that Jesus is the pattern His followers should imitate: "He who says he abides in Him ought himself to walk just as He walked (1 John 2:6).

Does this not lend the Sabbath day to moral obligation and perpetuity in the New Covenant era?

Exhibit D: Capital punishment was required for the violation of moral law.

Under the theocracy of Israel, God determined that willful violation of several of the Ten Commandments would be punishable by death. These included idolatry (Deuteronomy 13:6–15), blasphemy (Leviticus 24:16), adultery, same sex relations, and sexual relations with animals (Leviticus 20:10–16; Exodus 22:19–22), rebellion against parents (Leviticus 20:9), murder (Exodus 21:12–17), and defiling the Sabbath (Exodus 31:14, 15; Numbers 15:35).

Thus, capital punishment had to do with moral law—the fourth commandment Sabbath law included. It is moral law that defines sin (Romans 3:20; 7:7), and the wages of sin is death (Romans 6:23).

This evidence shows that the fourth commandment is a moral obligation before the Creator God.

Exhibit **E**: Jesus viewed the Sabbath as having been made for every person—Jew and Gentile.

That Jesus viewed the weekly Sabbath as all-inclusive is evident in His response to His detractors: " 'The Sabbath was made for man [Greek, *anthropos*, generic humanity] . . .' " (Mark 2:27, 28). As its originator, Jesus is stating a universal reality even as He was speaking universally—and not just for Jews—when He spoke about "a man" (also *anthropos*) leaving father and mother and clinging to his wife (Mark 10:7). From our first parents to the last person born on earth, all urgently need the seventh-day Sabbath as designed by Jesus in the Creation.

Jesus defined and lived the Sabbath as a day in time. It was a measure of time that was "blessed" and "sanctified" at Creation (Genesis 2:1–3). There is no record in Scripture of any pronouncement that this blessedness has been withdrawn or nullified. Therefore, it is still valid today—just as God intended.

There is no record after Christ's resurrection of His redefining the Sabbath as an existential experience removing the dimension of time—the seventh-day. Proof of this is in the fact that the infant church continued to keep the seventh day sacred, as has been shown earlier. The early Christian church found it safe to follow the pattern Jesus lived, as well as the example of the disciples who knew Jesus' heart most intimately. It is for this "faith once delivered" that Jude urges believers in every succeeding age to contend (Jude 3).

Exhibit **F**: God Himself specifically distinguished between the weekly Sabbath and the feast sabbaths:

And the LORD spoke to Moses saying, . . . "These are the feasts [which had their corresponding sabbaths] of the LORD which you shall proclaim to be holy convocations,

to offer an offering made by fire to the LORD, a burnt offering and a grain offering, a sacrifice and drink offerings,
everything on its day—*besides the* Sabbaths of the LORD."
(Leviticus 23:33, 37, 38, emphasis supplied)

In addition to the fourth commandment, spoken by God at Mt.
Sinai, the obligation to observe the weekly Sabbath of the fourth
commandment is mentioned in Exodus five times apart from the
feast sabbaths: (1) Exodus 16:4–30, (2) Exodus 23:12, (3) Exodus
31:13–18, (4) Exodus 34:21, and (5) Exodus 35:1, 2.

When Moses reminded the people of their duty to keep the Ten
Commandments in Deuteronomy, he included the fourth commandment Sabbath day (Deuteronomy 5:6–22). No "feast" sabbaths
are mentioned in the Ten Commandments.

From the beginning of their existence as a nation, the Israelites,
and later the Jewish people, have treated the weekly Sabbath as a
moral entity of the Ten Commandments. So did Jesus, His disciples
and the first century church.

Exhibit G: The early Christian church viewed the Ten Commandments as morally binding.

Did Christ's disciples and the wider congregation of followers of
Jesus in the early Christian church view the Ten Commandments as
morally binding?

Following the Day of Pentecost the Jerusalem church was made
up of the twelve disciples, the seven deacons, Nicodemus, Joseph
of Arimathea, a great company of priests who believed (Acts 6:7), a
portion of believing Pharisees (Acts 15:5) and a host of Jewish converts from the day of Pentecost. Their numbers increased daily. This
multitude of believers was considered by some in the Jewish hierarchy as heretics or dissidents from the Jewish faith and were called the
"minim."

Jewish author Aharon Oppenheimer called attention to evidence
about the regard these early Christians had for the Ten Commandments, which they referred to as the *mitzvot*:

This was the view of the early church, as we see from the Jewish reaction to the early church's view of the Decalogue. The minim [Hebrew for "heretics," a term used by some in the Jewish community to describe believers in Christ], both the Christians and the Jewish-Christian sects, stressed the universal foundation in the mitzvot [commandments] in the Torah, rather than the practical mitzvot, but *gave special importance to the Ten Commandments*, which continued to be binding, including those between God and mankind. As a result of this, the rabbis cancelled the saying of the Ten Commandments together with the paragraphs of the Shema prayer, so that no-one should mistakenly think that the mitzvot included in the Ten Commandments were more binding than the rest of the mitzvot in the Torah, as the minim claimed. (Aharon Oppenheimer, "Removing the Decalogue," *The Decalogue in Jewish and Christian Tradition*, 2011, p. 99, emphasis supplied)

Exhibit H: The Sabbath commandment is strategically placed among the Ten Commandments.

Three commandments precede the Sabbath commandment, and six commandments follow after it (Exodus 20:3–17). Why is the fourth commandment at the very heart of the Ten and by its content deemed central, strategic and perpetual throughout time?

(1) The Sabbath commandment stipulates that the originator of the earth and humanity is the Creator God. (2) It outlines the weekly cycle and designates time for work and time for rest—the seventh day of the week. (3) It affirms the social order of the family unit—husband and wife, son and daughter. (4) It designates the Creator as Sovereign of the universe. (5) It calls the human family to the primary purpose of existence—holiness to God. (6) It displays God's majesty and wisdom in His created works. (7) It promises blessedness (the favor and lavishness of God) to the participant.

The fourth commandment uniquely begins with the word "remember." There are many times for "remembering"—birthdays, anniversaries, reunions, the Fourth of July, Thanksgiving. These are yearly memorials of stellar events of the past and social checkpoints in human life. So it is that the Sabbath is a strategic weekly reminder to all people everywhere that they are the handiwork of the Creator God and are welcomed into His presence to continually experience His love and favor.

Human existence has a noble starting point, but it is an ever-present reality. We are all a part of this creation journey! Again and again we are drawn to be in awe of Him! The frequency of the Sabbath day—every week—shows the Creator's priority to make Himself known to humanity.

Jesus summarized the Ten Commandments as "love"—love to God and love to humanity (Matthew 22:36–4). But our love to humanity—to one another—can only exist when there is a genuine love and respect for God. Since humans are made in the "image of God" (Genesis 1:27), it is our distinct privilege to know and experience Him and to emulate His character.

God is a lover of people; His primary focus is fellowship with humans in intimate, personal relationship. God uses the most endearing social terminology to describe this intimacy. He portrays Himself as a husband (Isaiah 54:5, 6) and as a bridegroom (Matthew 25:1). He describes redeemed humanity as His wife (Revelation 19:7).

It should, therefore, come as no surprise that the fourth commandment comes before the last six commandments. When we have an ongoing, loving relationship with God, we will treasure the family (fifth commandment), we will guard and have sensitive respect for life and healthful living (sixth commandment), we will respect God's parameters for sexuality (seventh commandment), we will have regard for what rightly belongs to another (eighth commandment), we will pursue truth and truthfulness (ninth commandment), and we will exhibit an attitude of giving and wanting the best for others, guarding us against envy and unwholesome desire (tenth commandment).

Thus, the Sabbath commandment serves as part of the righteous foundation for social morality.

Exhibit I: The Sabbath is New Covenant morality.

That God views the fourth commandment as moral law can be seen in His personal warning to the wayward temple priests who were contemporaries of the prophet Ezekiel: " 'Her priests have violated My law and profaned My holy things; . . . they have hidden their eyes from My Sabbaths, so that I am profaned among them' " (Ezekiel 22:26).

The phrase "My law" is linked with "My Sabbaths"—seventh-day Sabbaths of the fourth commandment. It is God Himself who is speaking. With this in mind, it must be noted that this phraseology—"My law"—is repeated in the New Covenant that is ratified by the blood of Jesus in the New Testament: " 'I will put *My laws* in their mind and write them on their hearts; . . .' " (Hebrews 8:10, emphasis supplied). Again it is God who is speaking, and He does not exclude the fourth commandment—His "permanent imprint in time."

The fourth commandment transcends any ceremonial—temporary label. The weekly Saturday Sabbath is moral law and serves its ongoing strategic purpose in humanity's relationship with the Creator God. Why, then, should something as awe-inspiring and delightful as this sacred time with God not be a part of His New Covenant with redeemed humanity?

Exhibit J: The writers of the New Testament do not treat the Sabbath as ceremonial and temporary and, thereby, ending at the cross.

Matthew and Mark record the events that led up to Jesus' declaring Himself as LORD of the Sabbath (Matthew 12:8; Mark 2:27, 28). These events were written down several decades after the return of Jesus to the courts of heaven. What would have been the point in doing so if the Sabbath had already been discarded and replaced with Sunday worship?

Matthew records the concern that Jesus expressed about followers who would of necessity need to flee Jerusalem prior to its destruction: " 'And pray that your flight may not be in winter or on the Sabbath' " (Matthew 24:20). The historian Epiphanius notes that those followers of Jesus who fled from Jerusalem prior to its destruction continued to observe the Sabbath (*Panarion*, sect 29, chap. 7, verses 5, 7, 8).

Luke, the Gentile associate of Paul, wrote of the women who prepared the body of Jesus late on Friday after Jesus' death:

"Then they returned and prepared spices and oils. And they rested on the Sabbath according to the commandment" (Luke 23:56). Luke here confirmed the continuing status of the seventh-day Sabbath as Ten Commandment law—moral law. Gentile believers had no difficulty accepting the Sabbath day of which Jesus is LORD.

Matthew has preserved the record of Jesus' public confirmation of the permanence of the Law of God: " 'For assuredly, I say to you, till heaven and earth pass away, one jot or one tittle will by no means pass from the law till all is fulfilled' " (Matthew 5:18).

Luke recorded numerous occasions during Paul's evangelistic tours on which he taught and reasoned with Jews and Gentiles on the Sabbath (Acts 13:42, 44; 16:12, 13; 17:2; 18:4). Paul connects baptism with the resurrection of Jesus—not with Sunday observance (Romans 6:3–6).

In Christian and Jewish thinking, defiling the Sabbath was dishonorable. There is no mention of Sabbath violation in Paul's defense before his judges in Caesarea when he said: " '. . . Neither against the law of the Jews, nor against the temple, nor against Caesar have I offended in anything at all' "(Acts 25:8).

There is no requirement that any of the Ten Commandments be repeated in written form in the New Testament to authenticate their on-going relevance. (The truth is that none of the first four commandments are quoted in the New Testament, though they are affirmed in different ways.) Paul contrasts the changeable nature of circumcision with the "keeping of the commandments of God" (1 Corinthians 7:19). Jesus' righteous life of obedience to the law is the New Testament's affirmation of its continued permanence. It must be kept in mind that the Old Testament was the Scriptures of the infant church. The New Testament, as a collection of writings, would not be fully formed until after the death of the apostles.

It is in the New Testament that the relevance of the Ten Commandment law is shown to be an ever-present reality in the flow of human history: ". . . death spread to all men [to all humanity], because all sinned . . . but sin is not imputed when there is no law" (Romans 5:13).

It must be remembered that the Holy Spirit directed in the formation of these records written by inspired writers who were witnesses to the life of the first century church.

Exhibit K: Many Catholic and Protestant apologists categorize the fourth commandment as moral law.

One of the most widely recognized spokespersons for this view is Franklin Graham, son of Dr. Billy Graham, and director of the Billy Graham Evangelistic Association. In a public forum message he said:

> You say "What do you mean by sin? This is the new millennium; things have changed! We can do things today that we couldn't have done twenty-five or thirty years ago. Things are just different . . . we're more tolerant as a society!"
> Well, God's word doesn't change! [Audience gives sustained applause] God's laws, His standards are the same today as they are going to be a thousand years from now. God's law and His standards are forever.
>
> Do you want to know what sin is? Taking someone's life is a sin; abortion is murder; stealing is a sin against God; lying is a sin; worshiping idols is a sin; taking God's name in vain is a sin; not keeping the Sabbath day is a sin. (Franklin Graham, Spokane, Washington Festival, from a radio broadcast on the *Hour of Decision,* October 4, 2004)

Catholics view the decisions made at the Council of Trent (1546) as being authentic doctrinal positions of the Church. *The Catholic Encyclopedia* records Catholic teaching regarding the moral nature of the Sabbath commandment at that Council:

> The Church, on the other hand, after changing the day of rest from the Jewish Sabbath, or seventh day of the week, to the first, made the Third Commandment refer to Sunday as the day to be kept holy as the LORD's Day. The Council of Trent (sess. VI, can. xix) condemns those who deny that the Ten Commandments are binding on Christians.

("Commandments of God," *The Catholic Encyclopedia*, vol. 4, The Universal Knowledge Foundation, Inc., New York, 1913, p. 153)

EVIDENCE **#4**. The Sabbath was intended for the Gentiles.

Many assume that Gentiles are exempt from the Sabbath. Yet, are Gentiles exempt from obligation to the moral law of the Ten Commandments? Was the Sabbath an unnecessary expectation for non-Jews before and after the cross? When it comes to salvation, were Gentiles beyond the reach of "good news" prior to the cross? None of the prophets upheld the exclusivity of the Jews. In fact, Isaiah declared that the LORD would bring light to the Gentiles, and Israel was to be God's messenger:

"It is too small a thing that You should be My Servant to raise up the tribes of Jacob, and to restore the preserved ones of Israel; I will also give You as a light to the Gentiles, that You should be My salvation to the end of the earth.

"Thus says the LORD, the Redeemer of Israel, their Holy One; to Him whom man despises, to him whom the nation abhors, to the Servant of rulers: 'Kings shall see and arise, princes also shall worship, because of the LORD who is Faithful, the Holy One of Israel; and He has chosen You.' " (Isaiah 49:6, 7; see also Isaiah 42:6; 61:9; 62:2; 66:12)

God promised Abraham that through him " '. . . all the families of the earth shall be blessed' " (Genesis 12:3). Through the prophet Haggai, God explained that the coming Messiah was not the exclusive hope of the Israelites:

"And I will shake all nations, and they shall come to the Desire of All Nations [Jesus], and I will fill this temple with glory," says the LORD of hosts. (Haggai 2:7; see also Micah 4:2, 3; and Zephaniah 2:11)

Jeremiah also said: ". . . The Gentiles shall come to You from the ends of the earth and say, 'Surely our fathers have inherited lies. Worthlessness and unprofitable things.' Will a man make gods for himself, which are not gods?" (Jeremiah 16:19, 20).

Jesus' strategy was to break down the deep-seated, mistaken prejudice of the disciples toward Gentiles. The believing Magi from the East came to honor Him at His birth (Matthew 2:1–12). In the presence of His disciples, Jesus affirmed the Canaanite woman: " 'O woman, great is your faith! Let it be as you desire' " (Matthew 15:28). Jesus acknowledged the Roman centurion, who embraced the superiority of the God of the Jews, before an onlooking crowd, when He said: " 'I say to you, I have not found such great faith, not even in Israel!' " (Luke 7:9) Jesus then said: " '. . . many will come from the east and the west, and sit down with Abraham, Isaac, and Jacob in the kingdom of heaven' " (Matthew 8:11). After winning the heart of the Samaritan woman at the well, Jesus enlarged upon the possibilities to His disciples: " '. . . lift up your eyes and look at the fields, for they are already white for harvest!' " (John 4:35). While the religious elite cursed Jesus to His face upon the cross, it was the Gentile Roman executioner who with fear declared: " 'Truly this was the Son of God!' " (Matthew 27:54).

Even though witnessing the above encounters, Peter's prejudice remained. The Holy Spirit's conviction, which was brought upon the Roman centurion Cornelius and his household, opened the eyes of the disciple Peter, declaring that God is no respecter of persons (Acts 10:28). In the nighttime visit with Sanhedrin member Nicodemus, Jesus revealed the heart of God for Gentiles and Jews:

For God so loved the world that He gave His only begotten Son, that whosoever believes in Him should not perish but have everlasting life. (John 3:16)

For centuries the Israelite nation, with whom God had deposited the spiritual treasures of heaven in the written Word of God, stood at the crossroads of the nations for the specific purpose of winning the world to the Creator God. Through the prophet Isaiah, God commanded:

"Arise, shine; For your light has come! And the glory of the Lord is risen upon you . . . The Gentiles shall come to your light, and kings to the brightness of your rising. Lift up your eyes all around, and see: they all gather together, they come to you; your sons shall come from afar, and your daughters shall be nursed at your side . . ." (Isaiah 60:1–4)

One thousand years before Christ, King Solomon hosted the Queen of Sheba in Jerusalem. The queen returned to northern Africa with the spiritual treasures of Israel. Among them was the seventh-day Sabbath, which survived in northern Africa for centuries thereafter.

The prophet Jonah was sent to warn Nineveh, the heart of the Assyrian empire, about God's coming judgment upon their wickedness. Miraculously, the city repented. Five hundred years before Christ, God used the prophet Daniel to humble King Nebuchadnezzar of Babylon to acknowledge Him, the God of heaven (Daniel 4).

Isaiah, the Old Testament gospel prophet, recorded God's purposes:

"For my house [Solomon's temple] shall be called a house of prayer for all people." (Isaiah 56:7)

God's desires were even bigger than anyone expected:

"Do not let the son of the foreigner who has joined himself to the Lord speak, saying, 'The Lord has utterly separated me from His people'; nor let the eunuch say 'Here I am, a dry tree.' For thus says the Lord: To the eunuchs who keep My Sabbaths, and choose what pleases Me, and hold fast My covenant, Even them I will give My house and within My walls a place and a name . . .

"Also the sons of the foreigner who join themselves to the Lord, to serve Him, and to love the name of the Lord to be His servants—everyone who keeps from defiling the Sabbath, and holds My covenant—even them I will bring to My holy mountain and make them joyful in My house

of prayer. Their burnt offerings and their sacrifices will be accepted on My altar . . ." (Isaiah 56:3–7)

Isaiah challenged Judah and Israel to fulfill God's design. His prophetic ministry was among God's final appeals to the northern nation of Israel before she disappeared into captivity. What was Isaiah's fate? If tradition is to be trusted, his countrymen forced him into a hollow log and sawed him in two (a fate hinted at in Hebrews 11:37).

With this historical background and the initiation of the New Covenant ministry of Paul to the Gentile world, we must ask: *Did Gentile believers observe the Sabbath? What do the Scriptures say about Sabbath observance under grace?*

And when the Jews went out of the synagogue, the Gentiles *begged* that these words might be preached to them *the next Sabbath*. Now when the congregation had broken up, many of the Jews and devout proselytes followed Paul and Barnabas, who, speaking to them, persuaded them to continue in the *grace of God*. And *the next Sabbath* almost the whole city came together to hear the word of God. (Acts 13:42–44, emphasis supplied)

At the first church council at Jerusalem, the Sabbath was not questioned. Rather, it was taken for granted (Acts 15:21). After the council at Jerusalem, Paul and his missionary team came to Philippi, a Roman colony, which was without a Jewish synagogue. Even without a formal place of worship, Paul sought out a place where "prayer was customarily made" on the Sabbath. Down by the river, Paul found Gentile believers observing the Sabbath. Among them was Lydia, a Gentile seller of purple, who "worshiped God." Her heart was open to hear Paul's words:

And on the Sabbath day we went out of the city to the riverside, where prayer was customarily made; and we sat down and spoke to the women who met there. (Acts 16:13, 14)

While Paul was in the city of Corinth, God revealed to him that He had "much people in this city" (Acts 18:10). During the year and six months that Paul remained in the city, he preached to both Jews and Gentiles every Sabbath:

And he reasoned in the synagogue every Sabbath, and persuaded both Jews and Greeks. (Acts 18:4)

As time progressed in the coming centuries, the Christian church expanded rapidly among non-Jewish populations in Ireland and England, Europe, Asia Minor, Persia, India and the Far East. Thus, it could be said by church historian Socrates Scholasticus in the fifth century:

For although most all churches throughout the world celebrate the sacred mysteries [the LORD's Supper] on the Sabbath of every week, yet the Christians of Alexandria and Rome, on account of some ancient tradition, refuse to do this. (*Ecclesiastical History*, bk. 5, chap. 22, p. 289)

Remember what Jesus said about sacred time being blessed from the Creation: "The Sabbath was made for man" (Mark 2:27, 28)— for humanity. All humans throughout time in every corner of the earth need what God prepared at the Creation and proclaimed in the fourth commandment, which He engraved in stone.

Jewish author Abraham Heschel has reasoned that since "time" comes to everyone, the Sabbath is not to be observed only by one nation, sect, or class. Rather its blessings and obligations are universal and ageless.

Through the prophet Isaiah, The LORD would confirm this:

"For as the new heavens and the new earth. . . shall remain before me. . . from one Sabbath to another, *all flesh* shall come to worship before Me," says the LORD. (Isaiah 66:22, 23, emphasis supplied)

EVIDENCE #5. The Sabbath is the sign and seal of God.

Why would it matter if the fourth commandment were removed from the ten?

The Creator God declared the seventh-day Sabbath to be His "sign." He described it as "My holy day" (Isaiah 58:13). Upon it He placed His blessing, and in it He promises His presence. He said its sacredness is "perpetual" and "eternal." Its on-going reality is God's assurance that He—the LORD God, the Creator of mankind—is forever committed to His human family.

. . . I gave them my Sabbaths, to be a sign between them and Me, that they might know that I am the LORD who sanctifies them. (Ezekiel 20:12)

As a wedding ring and vows are given to declare a promise of commitment in marriage, so does God give His Sabbath to encircle His people as a sign that He has set them apart for holiness (Ezekiel 20:12). He is their King, their Protector and Provider. His love is the deepest and most devoted. His plans reach into eternity for those who join themselves to Him (Isaiah 56:6).

To be "sanctified" by God is to be cut away from sin's autonomous, independent self-centeredness. "Sanctified" living is the freedom to experience growing maturity in the righteousness of Christ, which comes by faith. To "rest" in the LORD's sacred time is to acknowledge His sovereignty and His will for one's life. It is a declaration that salvation is by trusting in the merits of Christ rather than in human effort or behavior.

What vital role does the fourth commandment contribute to the Ten Commandment document? Take a close look. Note this strategic feature: it is a statement of authorship and the certification of God's authority.

The fourth commandment, distinguished from the other nine, contains what the others do not have—the underlying credentials upon which God has the right and authority to morally obligate the human family to live all ten commandments. He is distinguished in the fourth commandment by His seal as the sovereign and living Creator God. It contains His name—the LORD God Jehovah, His title—the Creator, and His domain—heaven and earth (Exodus 20:8–10). Is this not unlike the "presidential" seal?

Alter, remove, replace, or ignore the Creator's sacred time, and what then would be done? What attitude would that reveal before the living God?

Jesus will always be the "LORD even of the Sabbath." In the context of the seventh day being His "sign" and "seal" of Sovereignty, what does it mean to "put on Christ"? That is for you to determine.

Like a suitor making a date with his beloved, it is a command that is full of promise and blessing. Second guessing is not required; the appointed time is specific—it is the seventh day. Is the Creator's designated "sacred time" with humanity no longer of value in the twenty-first century? What does it mean when people continue to ignore their Maker's weekly date?

EVIDENCE #6. The Sabbath is a test.

Every person who is born on planet earth—from Adam and Eve to those living this very moment—is indebted to their Maker. Paul quoted the poet Epimenides in saying of God: "In Him we live and move and have our being" (Acts 17:28). Every heartbeat, every breath of air we take is an extension of His life-giving power.

Given this reality about life on earth, every person has an obligation from gratitude to trust and obey the commands of the Creator God. Few realize, however, that God's commands for wholesome living are actually the blossoms of promises, which, when obeyed, bloom into blessings. This means that God's commands are promises! On the other hand, people who decide to wantonly take matters into their own hands and ignore God's Ten Commandment law will also discover another promise—the resulting curse that comes from disobedience: "The way of the transgressor is hard" (Proverbs 13:15). Is this why today's world is filled with so much unhappiness?

Moses spelled out this formula for ancient Israel: Obey God's commands and be blessed; disobey God's commands and be cursed (Deuteronomy 28). At the end of his warnings, this great leader pleaded with his countrymen:

"I call heaven and earth as witnesses today against you, that I have set before you life and death, blessing and cursing; therefore choose life, that both you and your descendants may live; that you may love the Lord your God, that you may obey His voice, and that you may cling to Him, for He is your life and the length of your days; and that you may dwell in the land which the Lord swore to your fathers, to Abraham, Isaac, and Jacob, to give them." (Deuteronomy 29:19, 20)

Indeed, Abraham would become the prime example of the kind of relationship that God wants with every human being. Abraham came to know and trust God to the degree that he could *take God at His word without questioning*. He truly believed that every command from God was a promise that would translate into blessing.

At God's command to offer his son Isaac as a sacrifice, Abraham proceeded to trustingly journey to Mount Moriah where he built an altar to worship God. Out of trust for his father and his father's God, Isaac was willing to be placed as a sacrifice upon the altar. As Abraham raised the knife to plunge it into his son, the Lord intervened. The Bible says God was testing Abraham (Genesis 22:1). A heavenly messenger called:

"Do not lay your hand on the lad or do anything to him; for now I know that you fear God, seeing you have not withheld your son, your only son, from Me." (Genesis 22:12)

Abraham had shown by his actions that he *took God at His word*. His obedience to God's commands brought him the title "the friend of God." It demonstrated once again that every command of God is a promise that God will turn into a blessing. So what was the blessing? It was the forecast of the coming Savior of the world! This story has become the heritage of millions of people through the ages, illustrating the ultimate sacrifice the heavenly Father would make in giving His Son—His only Son—Jesus.

Four hundred years later, the children of Israel experienced the mighty hand of God delivering them from Egypt. By faith they obeyed His command—they placed the blood of a lamb upon their doorposts, and the death angel passed over every house where the blood had been placed. This is why the celebration was called the "Passover." The Israelites were now being formed into a nation that would extend the noble example and the "everlasting covenant" of Abraham—their forefather.

The LORD wanted to demonstrate before the nations of the world that a whole nation could trust Him even as Abraham had. So it happened that God would test them weeks prior to the giving of the Ten Commandment law at Mt. Sinai. The account continues:

Then the LORD said to Moses, "Behold, I will rain bread from heaven for you. And the people shall go out and gather a certain quota every day, that I may test them, whether they will walk in My law or not . . ." (Exodus 16:4)

God now commanded that on the sixth day of the week, a double portion of manna should be gathered. Yet, on the seventh day—on the LORD's Sabbath—none should be gathered.

Remember, God's commands are promises. In this instance the blessing was that God would perform a miracle. Though no manna would fall on the Sabbath, the double portion gathered on the sixth day would do that which it would not do on any other day, it would be preserved for food over the seventh day.

How did they respond to the test? Did all Israel *take God at His word?*

Now it happened that some of the people went out on the seventh day to gather, but they found none. And the LORD said to Moses, "How long do you refuse to keep My commandments and My laws?" (Exodus 16:28)

The Creator God had chosen the Sabbath to test His people. That the Sabbath was not new to Israel is implied in God's question: "How long do you refuse . . .?" How long would it be for Israel to learn to *take God at His word* even as Abraham had?

For the next forty years, no manna would fall on the seventh day. Every week, from that point forward, God would perform the same Sabbath miracle. No one in Israel would ever make the mistake again of thinking that they could pick and choose whichever day they wanted for "rest from labor." God had spoken.

A final test for Judah

Less than one thousand years later, what was left of God's people—the nation of Judah—had given themselves over to chronic idolatry. The kingdom of Babylon had already taken many of Judah's best sons and daughters into exile. Judah was sliding quickly toward destruction.

The last four kings of Judah did wickedness before the LORD. God called three prophets—Ezekiel, Jeremiah and Daniel—to proclaim His warnings to Judah. The LORD judges the attitude of the leaders and the people toward Himself by the way they treat His prophets. The on-site prophet, Jeremiah, was completely scorned. He was thrown into prison, exiled to Egypt and later confined to a pit in Jerusalem.

Ezekiel was exiled to Babylon. Through him God exposed the serious offenses of Judah's religious leaders in their backslidden condition. Ezekiel declared:

"Her priests have violated My law and profaned My holy things; they have not distinguished between the holy and unholy, nor have they made known the difference between the unclean and the clean; and they have hidden their eyes from My Sabbaths [fourth commandment], so that I am profaned among them." (Ezekiel 22:26)

The destructive forces of the Babylonian army were now on their way to demolish Jerusalem's walls and the king's palaces. Everything was at stake, including the world-renowned temple of Solomon, the very house of God. God would spare Judah and the city from this crushing blow if Judah would respond to her Protector's final test. Jeremiah publicly announced:

". . . Hear the word of the Lord, you kings of Judah, and all Judah, and all the inhabitants of Jerusalem . . . Take heed to yourselves, and bear no burden on the Sabbath day, nor bring it in by the gates of Jerusalem; nor carry a burden out of your houses on the Sabbath day, nor do any work, but hallow the Sabbath day, as I commanded your fathers." (Jeremiah 17:20–22)

God's chosen instrument of examination was the fourth commandment, which contains His seal of sovereignty. This makes it His sign. Now it had become the supreme test of Judah's loyalty once again. This time God announced through Jeremiah what would happen if Judah failed to exercise their choice to *take God at His word:*

"But if you will not heed Me to hallow the Sabbath day, such as not carrying a burden when entering the gates of Jerusalem on the Sabbath day, then I will kindle a fire in its gates, and it shall devour the palaces of Jerusalem, and it shall not be quenched." (Jeremiah 17:27)

Blinded by years of unfaithfulness, the princes, priests, and people gave this sad, fateful response to their sovereign and heavenly King:

And they said, "This is hopeless! So we will walk according to our own plans, and we will every one do the imagination of his evil heart." (Jeremiah 18:12)

When the people of God seek the delight and blessing of the Sabbath experience, they reveal their reliance and dependence on God's wisdom and protection. In this case, Judah collectively demonstrated an autonomous attitude of chronic indifference and defiance toward their Provider. The Sabbath directive from God served as a barometer of the heart. The actions of the leaders of Judah had revealed that they no longer recognized God's dominion over them.

The people of Judah had sealed their fate. Soon the Shekinah glory would withdraw from the Most Holy Place of Solomon's temple, linger over the Mount of Olives, as if loath to leave, then completely vanish. Then the armies of Babylon would wreak their cruel havoc unhindered.

Ancient Judah foolishly lost Jerusalem, their nation in disarray for having lost her sense of conscious obligation to the Creator God. It is ironic that six hundred years later Jewish leaders would again watch Jerusalem and its second temple being destroyed by the armies of Rome. This time it would be for rejecting the LORD of the Sabbath.

More ironic still, 250 years later, Christendom failed its own Sabbath test, as leaders of the church promoted another day under the pretense of exalting Christ and, consciousness of seventh-day "sacred time," watched the Sabbath fade into the shadows like a stranger un-remembered.

God's tests are real, and they have had real-world consequences that have continued to the present.

EVIDENCE #7. The Sabbath shows trust in God's word.

It was in the Garden of Eden that our first parents came to know God. Their first full day on earth—the seventh day—was spent as sacred time, resting in the presence of their Creator (Genesis 2:1–3).

In the course of time, Adam and Eve faced a test that is common to all humans. Would they *take God at His word*, or would they rely on their own inclination? The issue at stake was *trust*. Would the love that God had shown and the relationship they had formed sustain their conscience as a defense against the subtleties of an enemy in disguise? In love God had created them with free will. It was for them to choose, though the consequences were enormous—either life or death!

Near the tree of life, which was in the middle of the garden, stood the tree of the knowledge of good and evil. To Adam and Eve God gave the command:

"Of every tree of the garden you may freely eat; but of the tree of the knowledge of good and evil you shall not eat, for in the day that you eat of it you shall surely die." (Genesis 2:16, 17)

The tree God designated untouchable was a fruit-bearing tree like any other in paradise. It took its nutrients from the same soil, was watered from the same underground fountains, and filtered the breezes in the same way as any tree in the garden. The fruit of this tree was not fatally poisonous. The eye could gaze upon its God-created beauty with delight. Reason alone would conclude that its fruit would be delicious—even exhilarating. The only feature that distinguished this tree from the others was that which God Himself had said—"You will not eat of it or you *will die!*"

It was at this tree in the Garden of Eden that the LORD allowed limited access by His enemy, a rival intelligent angel in rebellion against God.

This enemy, his true form and identity disguised, offered a mellow whisper of doubt about what God had said. Was God keeping something from Adam and Eve? Taken in by the voice of this stranger, Eve chose to doubt and distrust her Maker. She failed to *take God at His word.*

The rest of the story is well known to the generations that have followed. Yet, the test is as real today as it was then—will humans be content to believe and trust God? Will they *take God at His word* or will they take life into their own hands, relying on their own self-centered works and reasoning apart from God?

In a similar way, by all external appearances, the seventh day of the weekly cycle is just like any other twenty-four hour day. On it the sun may shine or stormy rain may fall. It can be icy cold or summer hot—all nature continues on in its cycle, the same as any other day. Nothing in the physical and celestial realm naturally distinguishes Saturday as being unique or special. It is only what the Creator God has said about the seventh day that makes it the crowning climax of each week. Of course, what God says makes all the difference! The Creator God has declared it sacred time to be remembered. Upon it He decreed "blessing" and "hallowedness" in permanent sequence through time (Genesis 2:1–3).

In God's way of thinking, the world's birthday is not an annual celebration—it is weekly. Fifty-two days a year are declared a sacred vacation with God Himself, as author Don Postema has described it:

The sabbath is a gift from God given to humanity from the beginning . . . A vacation with God planned from the beginning to be enjoyed into eternity. (*Catch Your Breath:* God's Invitation to Rest, CRC Publications, Grand Rapids, Michigan, 1997, p. 15)

The Sabbath day's signature of authenticity is that the Creator has declared it to be so (Exodus 20:8–11). He spoke, and it was done (Psalm 33:8, 9).

Again, it is so only because God said it is so. The Sabbath command is from the Creator to the creature. On other issues, scientists conduct tests to prove a hypothesis, and lawyers argue a case to persuade beyond "reasonable doubt." Yet, with the Sabbath, the Creator's command is all that is needed.

For the one who observes the Sabbath of the LORD, it is a pure act of trust and faith—*taking God at His word* (Hebrews 11:1–3). Because it is an arbitrary command (though weekly rest does make sense), it provides a true indicator of one's willingness to acknowledge that God is the sovereign LORD.

Theologian Raoul Dederen explains:

As the Christian takes heed of the Sabbath day and keeps it holy, he does so purely in answer to God's command, and simply because God is his Creator. Thus, the Sabbath command comes nearer to being a true measure of spirituality than any other of the commandments, and, as in the days of Israel of old, it is often more of a test of loyalty to God than is any of the others. To be willing on the Sabbath day to withdraw from the tyranny of the world of things in order to meet the LORD of heaven and earth in the quiet of our souls means to love God with all our hearts, souls, minds, and bodies. (*The Sabbath in Scripture and History,* Review & Herald Publishing Assoc., Hagerstown, Maryland, 1982, p. 302)

In this discourse we have reflected on the issue that divides worldwide Christianity: *Should tradition and Scripture be treated as equal part-*

ners in spiritual truth, and should human ecclesiastical choices, which override God's expressed will, be allowed to govern individual conscience? The Creation Sabbath has a unique bearing on these questions. Biblical Research Institute professor E. Edward Zinke wrote:

In principle, it [the Sabbath] encompasses humanity's entire relationship with God. The Sabbath holds together the past, present and future. It testifies that God has acted on the behalf of His people in the past, that He is acting on their behalf in the present and that He will act for them in the future. Those who willingly acknowledge the LORD of the Sabbath by doing so also acknowledge the sovereignty of God's Word. The Sabbath is thus an arbitrary tree of knowledge of good and evil in the midst of the garden. It is a test of and a witness to true allegiance to the God of the universe. (*Perspective Digest,* vol. 5, no. 4 [2000], pp. 27, 28)

If the Sabbath of Creation is a modern tree of knowledge of good and evil, should we not expect to hear somewhere near, the voice of another "stranger" whose real identity is disguised and whose subtle whispers entice humanity to doubt and disregard the Creator's command?

Based on a prophetic vision, the prophet Daniel described a "little horn" power that would establish dominion over the nations. Daniel's attention was especially drawn, in this same vision, to the "little horn" because it had "eyes like the eyes of a man, and a mouth speaking pompous words" (Daniel 7:8). A heavenly being identified for Daniel the entity's daring actions:

He shall speak pompous words against the Most High, shall persecute the saints of the Most High, and shall intend to change times and law. The saints shall be given into his hand for a time and times and half a time. (Daniel 7:25)

Has Bible prophecy come to fulfillment as seen from our vantage point in the flow of history? Has an "empire" claiming spiritual authority over the nations boasted of changing God's law, including "time"? Documented evidence from history tells what took place.

Is there a modern equivalent to the tree of the knowledge of good and evil that will test each person as to whether or not they will *take God at His word*? And will the consequences ultimately be the same—life or death?

Again, you decide.

EVIDENCE #8. The Sabbath reveals Christ's righteousness.

When Jesus came to the Jordan River to be baptized, John the Baptist acknowledged his unworthiness to serve with baptism One who was so pure and holy. Jesus' answer to John gave not only the reason He should be baptized but also the mission of His life:

> **Permit it to be so now, for thus it is fitting for us to fulfill all righteousness.** (Matthew 3:15)

In a world saturated with sin, Jesus came, not only to have "laid on Him the iniquity of us all" in His infinite sacrifice of death on the cross, but to live a perfectly righteous, sinless life. Since Adam—and to this very day—no one but Jesus has lived such a life.

It is this perfect life that qualifies Jesus as the Son of God to be "the LORD our righteousness," as the prophet Jeremiah called Him (Jeremiah 23:6).

Jesus lived a life of honor to His heavenly Father and perfectly carried out His will. " '. . . I always do those things that please Him' " (John 8:29), He declared.

In this way, Jesus' life of righteous obedience recovered what Adam and Eve had lost through sin. The Apostle Paul makes this comparison:

> **For as by one man's disobedience many were made sinners, so also by one Man's obedience many will be made righteous.** (Romans 5:19)

It is perfect obedience that the righteous Ten Commandment law of God requires. This is the "gold standard" of righteous living. Yet, it is obvious, that of all who have ever lived—

. . . there is none righteous, no, not one; . . . for all have sinned and come short of the glory of God. (Romans 3:10, 23)

The good news of the gospel is that by faith the repentant sinner may be credited (imputed) with the righteous, obedient life of Jesus Christ. That which humans do not have to give—perfect obedience—is provided by Jesus. This is amazing grace! It is true that humans are not only saved by Jesus' death on the cross but also that ". . . we shall be saved by His life" (Romans 5:10). Together, this is the experience of "justification by faith" (Romans 1:17).

In the experience of sanctification, the obedient, righteous life of Jesus is also to be lived out or "imparted" in the life of the believer:

. . . whoever keeps [treasures] His word, truly the love of God is perfected in him. By this we know that we are in Him. He who says he abides in Him ought himself also to walk just as He walked. (1 John 2:5, 6; see also Galatians 2:20)

Even the power to live the obedient, Christ-like life is provided to the believer. It is through the indwelling Spirit of Christ (Romans 8:11).

The moment before Jesus died on the cross, He cried out in victory, " 'It is finished!' " (John 19:30). Of course, that which was successfully completed was the divine plan laid before the foundation of the world to pay in full the debt of humanity's sin. Also completed was the life-long mission of Jesus to "fulfill all righteousness." Jesus' sinless, righteous life is the Ten Commandment law lived without a flaw. Jesus is the Ten Commandments in living, human form.

Now we must ask: *What is the righteousness of Christ that is in the fourth commandment that Jesus lived out perfectly and that will be credited to the account of every repentant believer?*

Since He claims to have kept God's commandments in full (John 15:10), it is consistent to conclude that the seventh-day Sabbath, lived out perfectly by Jesus, is credited to the account of every repentant believer as Christ's righteousness.

And what is the righteous experience in the fourth commandment, modeled by Jesus, that the Holy Spirit empowers His disciples in every age to live out in real life? The fourth commandment says:

Remember the Sabbath day to keep it holy. Six days you shall labor and do all your work, but the seventh day is the Sabbath of the LORD your God. In it you shall do no work: . . . For in six days the LORD made the heavens and the earth, the sea, and all that is in them, and rested the seventh day. Therefore the LORD blessed the Sabbath day and hallowed it. (Exodus 20:8–11)

This expresses the on-going will of the Father as lived out by the Son. It is part of His last will and testament, sealed in His dying cry on the cross—" 'It is finished.' " Nothing needed to be added; nothing should be taken away. No human can legitimately or legally alter a "last will and testament" after the person has died.

In Christ's perfect observance of the Sabbath throughout His life on earth, the fourth commandment Sabbath day was woven into the fabric of "the LORD OUR RIGHTEOUSNESS." Upon our Savior's death, this noble, honorable righteousness of Jesus was accepted and confirmed by all of heaven. Heaven's ratification resulted in the triumphal resurrection of Jesus from the tomb.

As Abraham believed God and it was counted to him as righteousness, so by faith can the righteousness of Jesus in keeping the fourth commandment be claimed by every believer. It is for you to choose.

Is Redemption linked to the Creation Sabbath?

From the Creation, our first parents happily reflected perfectly the moral qualities of their Maker. Their deepening fellowship and understanding of God were guaranteed, and they were commanded to be fruitful in extending these privileges and purity of character to their children.

Then Adam and Eve chose to believe the serpent's lie, and their moral character was compromised. They hid themselves, and the sentence of their extinction loomed imminent. But the Creator chose to give them what they did not deserve—grace. He promised them a substitute—a Deliverer who would take on the penalty in their place. For the very first time, the shedding of the blood of an innocent animal illustrated the coming Lamb of God who would take upon Himself the sin of every human being who would ever live on the planet. Redemption was now secured for anyone who, by faith and repentance, would claim the provision.

Is there then a link between the Creation Sabbath and humanity's redemption? The Apostle Paul stated it in these words: ". . . if anyone is in Christ, he is a *new creation* . . ." (2 Corinthians 5:17, emphasis supplied). Yes, through the new birth the repentant sinner may be credited with the moral purity of the Righteous One.

We now know that Jesus Christ our Creator is also the Passover Lamb our Mighty Deliverer. At His death on the cross, the thick temple curtain between the Holy and the Most Holy Place was supernaturally torn from top to bottom. The offering of the sacrificial lamb in the temple was interrupted. It was under a cloud of black darkness at mid-afternoon on Friday, the sixth day of the week, that the Creator completed His work of redemption. His precious, bleeding body was gathered to a borrowed tomb where He rested on the seventh day, which was a Sabbath. The Creation was redeemed in the identical weekly format—God rested on the seventh day both in Creation and in Redemption. This was not happenstance! Rather, it was the divine formula.

From the New Testament we can see that the seventh-day Sabbath has a dual divine intention—Creation and Redemption. "For you were bought at a price; therefore glorify God in your body and in your spirit, which are God's" (1 Corinthians 6:20).

In becoming the Passover Lamb, the Creator God became the Rescuing God. And this additional dimension to the Sabbath was first stated in an Old Testament reference to the fourth commandment:

"Observe the Sabbath day, to keep it holy, as the LORD your God commanded you. Six days you shall labor and do all your work, but the seventh day is the Sabbath of the LORD your God. . . .

"And remember that you were a slave in the land of Egypt, and that the LORD your God brought you out from there by a mighty hand and by an outstretched arm; therefore the LORD your God commanded you to keep the Sabbath day." (Deuteronomy 5:12–15)

Is not Israel's deliverance from Egypt a type of every sinner's deliverance from the slavery of sin?

Thus, it is not without notice that the writer of the book of Hebrews refers to God's "rest" on the seventh day (Hebrews 4:4), explaining that Israel, because of repeated disobedience, did not experience God's rest. Yet, "There remains therefore a rest [literally "Sabbath observance"] for the people of God [Jew and Gentile]. For he who has entered His rest has himself also ceased from his works as God did from His" (Hebrews 4:9, 10).

The author of Hebrews here declares that those who enter the Creation "Sabbath rest" established at the Creation, do so acknowledging their trust in the righteousness provided and credited to them by Christ rather than through the faultiness of human effort.

Why is this important? Many have viewed Sabbath-observance as mere legalism—as another means of meriting salvation. But in reality, it is the very opposite. The seventh-day Sabbath "rest" in the New Testament is a celebration of trust in the sufficiency of the righteousness of Jesus as the believer's assurance.

The wisdom of God in the reoccurring cycle of seventh-day Sabbaths from week to week not only reminds New Covenant believers regularly of their noble origin but provides an opportunity, out of personal conviction, to declare their trust in the merciful grace of God moment by moment, crediting them with the holy character of Jesus Christ. Sweet peace and rest indeed!

This is Jesus' invitation: " 'Come unto Me, all you who labor and are heavy laden, and I will give you rest. Take My yoke upon you and learn of Me, for I am gentle and lowly in heart, and you will find rest for your souls. For My yoke [of love] is easy and My burden is light' " (Matthew 11:28–30).

Amazingly, it is through the process of continually coming to Christ in response to this invitation that the believer will find his own life naturally becoming more like that of Jesus. And this is the objective for which the Sabbath is called God's sign:

"Moreover I also gave them My Sabbaths, to be a sign between them and Me, that they might know that I am the LORD who sanctifies them." (Ezekiel 20:12, 20)

EVIDENCE **#9**. The Sabbath reveals who it was that died on the cross.

One might think that Jesus' confrontations with Jewish religious leaders about the Sabbath day bore no relationship to His crucifixion. Yet, nearly every instance in which He came into conflict with the Pharisees over the Sabbath ended in the Jewish leaders' determination to have Him killed (Matthew 12:14 and Mark 3:6; Luke 6:11; John 5:18; 7:30).

Notice the reaction to Jesus' announcement as His being "LORD even of the Sabbath" (Matthew 12:8):

Then the Pharisees went out and took counsel, how they might destroy Him. (Matthew 12:14)

Yet, try as they might, they never found any solid evidence that Jesus actually broke the Sabbath. Each time they questioned Him, He successfully defended His actions and those of His disciples by Scriptural case law. As important as the Sabbath was to the Jews, hedged in by over 200 rabbinic laws, the subject of Jesus' Sabbath observance never came up in the record of His trial.

Was the Sabbath a vital link in Christ's journey to Calvary? What significance is there between the seventh day and this strategic moment in time?

Once during Jesus' ministry, when He and His disciples had fed themselves by plucking heads of grain on the Sabbath, Jesus announced to the objecting Pharisees: " 'But I say to you that in this place there is One greater than the temple' " (Matthew 12:6).

In the context of announcing Himself as the "LORD even of the Sabbath," Jesus was declaring Himself to be the Divine Creator. He was proclaiming that the One who made the Sabbath was in their midst.

Jesus continued on to the synagogue where He proceeded to visibly demonstrate His divine claim by healing the man with the withered hand. In so doing, Jesus was bringing authenticity to His divinity and sovereignty. This was not an isolated event. Does this not appear to be a calculated strategy on Jesus' part to show to the Jewish religious leaders that He was indeed the predicted Messiah of whom the prophets testified?

On another occasion, Jesus took the initiative to announce His divine nature within the context of a Sabbath healing. Surely the tangible evidence of a miracle would open the door of belief for their proud, stubborn hearts.

The thirty-eight year cripple

Jesus went to the pool of Bethesda, which was surrounded by the incurably sick. To the man who had a crippling malady for the previous thirty-eight years, Jesus said: " 'Do you want to be made well?' " (John 5:6).

Foreseeing that, once healed, this victim of paralysis would be confronted by the Sabbath "police," Jesus commanded the man: " 'Rise, take up your bed and walk' " (verse 8). Believing Jesus, the man acted upon His command. Jesus quietly disappeared into the crowd. Just as Jesus knew would happen, the newly healed man—carrying away his belongings with new vitality—was confronted by the Jews for violating the Sabbath. Rather than celebrate the man's moment of providence, their priority was the investigation of a "crime." Thus, they asked, " 'Who was the person who told you to take up your bed and walk?' "

At the temple, Jesus found the healed man and identified Himself to him. Note the Jews' response when the former cripple told them that it was Jesus who had made him well:

For this reason the Jews persecuted Jesus, and sought to kill him, because He had done these things on the Sabbath. (John 5:16)

When confronted by the Jews for this healing, Jesus defended Himself by bringing into focus the issue of His divinity and authoritative recreative power:

"My Father has been working until now, and I have been working. . . . For as the Father raises the dead and gives life to them, even so the Son gives life to whom He will. For the Father judges no one, but has committed all judgment to the Son, that all should honor the Son just as they honor the Father. He who does not honor the Son does not honor the Father who sent Him." (John 5:17, 19–47)

With these words, Jesus had now given His most comprehensive unfolding of His divine mission in union with His heavenly Father. His statement was bold, daring and straightforward. With it, He put the religious leaders on notice regarding who it was that they were opposing. Would they appreciate the great light given them? Would they rejoice that the Hope of Israel's existence had finally come? Would they embrace the tangible evidence just witnessed in the restoration of a chronically sick man? Note their distressing response:

Therefore the Jews sought all the more to kill Him, because He not only broke the Sabbath, but also said that God was His Father, making Himself equal with God. (John 5:18)

The stage had been set; it was now a matter of time. The seventh-day Sabbath of the fourth commandment had been forever linked with the reality of divinity in the person of Jesus Christ. The spiritual leaders in Jerusalem must be given time to ponder, observe, and formulate their response.

Once again, in the treasury of the temple in Jerusalem, the Jews entered into dispute with Jesus regarding His identity (John 8). Every line of Jesus' reasoning was to break through the darkness of their prejudice and pride.

Then they said to Him, "Who are You?" And Jesus said to them, "Just what I have been saying to you from the

beginning. . . . When you lift up the Son of Man, then you will know that I am He, and that I do nothing of Myself; but as My Father taught Me, I speak these things.'' (John 8:25, 28)

These temple leaders, claiming Abraham as their father (verse 41), now insinuated that Jesus had an illegitimate birth (verse 19), and they accused Him of being a Samaritan possessed of a demon.

The confrontation would come to an abrupt end when Jesus touched a sensitive nerve: " 'Your father Abraham rejoiced to see My day, and he saw it and was glad. . . . Most assuredly, I say to you, before Abraham was, I AM' '' (John 8:56, 58). In this statement, Jesus identified Himself with a name that only the God of Abraham, Isaac and Jacob would use—the great "I AM."

The temple leaders reacted immediately:

Then they took up stones to throw at Him; but Jesus hid Himself and went out of the temple, going through the midst of them, and so passed by. (John 8:59)

One last time Jesus would bring the Jewish leaders face to face with the issue of His identity as the Messiah of God. One last time, a Sabbath healing initiated the confrontation. Tradition and false theology about the Messiah had blinded the religious leaders to whom it was that they were bitterly opposing. One last time, Jesus would make His appeal.

Healing the man born blind

In the ninth chapter of John's Gospel is the celebrated story of the man who was born blind. When Jesus had answered the disciples' questions about why the man was born blind, Jesus did something very unusual—

He spat on the ground and made clay with the saliva and He anointed the eyes of the blind man with the clay. And He said to him, "Go wash in the pool of Siloam." . . . So he went and washed, and came back seeing. (John 9:6, 7)

115

When the man healed of blindness was brought to the Pharisees, he uttered a marvelous defense for Jesus:

"Since the world began it has been unheard of that anyone opened the eyes of one who was born blind. If this Man [Jesus] were not from God, He could do nothing." (John 9:32, 33)

The Pharisees received this statement with resentment and cast the man out of their presence. When Jesus heard that they had done this, He sought out the man, and this momentous conversation took place:

Jesus . . . said to him, "Do you believe in the Son of God?" He answered and said, "Who is He, LORD, that I may believe in Him?" And Jesus said to him, "You have both seen Him and it is He who is talking with you."

Then he said, "LORD, I believe!" And then he worshiped Him.

And Jesus said, "For judgment I have come into this world, that those who do not see may see, and that those who see may be made blind." (John 9:35–39)

The religious leaders again disputed with Jesus over His authority, demanding that Jesus tell them who He was. He plainly explained His mission to them, ending with the statement, "I and my Father are one" (John 10:30). What was their response?

Then the Jews took up stones again to stone Him . . . "For a good work we do not stone You, but for blasphemy, and because You, being a Man, make Yourself God." Therefore they sought again to seize Him, but He escaped out of their hand. (John 10:31, 33, 39)

Jesus answers the high priest

After Jesus' struggle in Gethsemane, He was arrested by the temple guard in the Valley of Kidron and brought to the house of Annas, the former High Priest. Immediately He was rushed before the High Priest Caiaphas and the illegally assembled Jewish Sanhedrin.

The temple palace of the High Priest was filled with the spirit of hatred and vengeance. False testimony was hurled at Jesus. He was jostled and spit upon with the vilest insults. Yet, Jesus maintained calm dignity; in silence He was approaching His hour of destiny. The scene was tense with an ominous sense of Jesus' fate.

The accusation was the same—Who are you, Jesus? At this climactic moment, Caiaphas stepped forward to press for his ends. Though it was illegal for the accused to incriminate Himself or stand trial without a defender—the High Priest impulsively placed Jesus under oath:

"I adjure You by the living God that You tell us if You are the Christ, the Son of God."

Jesus answered him, "It is as you said. Nevertheless, I say to you, hereafter you will see the Son of Man sitting at the right hand of the Power, and coming on the clouds of heaven." (Matthew 26:63, 64)

At this poignant answer, Caiaphas angrily tore his priestly robe, an impulsive act that, by tradition, disqualified him from serving as High Priest. " 'He has spoken blasphemy!' " raged Caiaphas. " 'He is deserving of death,' " came the collective voice of the Sanhedrin mob. Then they spit in Jesus' face with ridicule, beat Him and slapped Him with disdain.

Soon the cruel cry, " 'Crucify Him,' " echoed in Pilate's judgment hall. The leaders of the Jewish nation, including the High Priest, had irrationally rejected the LORD of the Sabbath. A fog of denial and a spirit of revulsion darkened their hearts and minds. The death sentence pronounced, the soldiers hurried Jesus to the place of execution.

When Jesus was nailed to the cross and hung dying with the burden of the sins of the whole world pressing upon Him, He did so totally abandoned by the Jewish hierarchy. Yet, even while hanging on the cross, Jesus received the affirmation of His divinity from both Jew and Gentile.

With words of belief, the Jewish thief appealed to Him: " 'LORD, remember me when You come into Your kingdom' " (Luke 23:42). Also, in awe and great fear, the Gentile executioner proclaimed: " 'Truly this was the Son of God!' " (Matthew 27:54).

What is the implication of this collection of true-to-life episodes recorded by the Gospel writers? Does it matter that the Sabbath of the fourth commandment was chosen by Jesus to put forth His divinity and sovereign authority? Is it not true that what Jesus said of Himself to the leaders of the Jewish nation, He is also saying to the rest of the world throughout time?

The fourth commandment Sabbath, of which Jesus declares Himself LORD, uniquely positions Jesus as Maker of the human family and the rightful Savior of every sinner. Within this commandment are Jesus' credentials as divine Sovereign: (1) the LORD God, (2) Maker, (3) of the heavens and earth (Exodus 20:8–11).

Is it reasonable to think that, following the anguish and ignominy of the cross, Jesus would now wish to retire the very institution that demonstrates His divine credentials, to surrender the very document containing the "sign" of His being the rightful Sovereign and Rescuer of Earth's inhabitants?

In the battle with His archenemy, would Jesus now relinquish the "sacred time" by which for thousands of years He has drawn human beings into intimate fellowship with Himself?

Furthermore, had the followers of Christ dismissed the seventh-day Sabbath after the Resurrection, would they not have unwittingly denigrated Christ's LORDship as Creator and undermined His sovereign right to pay in full the human debt of sin at the cross and to come forth victoriously from the tomb?

It is for you to make the call. . . .

In light of Jesus' several appeals to the Jewish leaders to declare His divinity and sovereign authority within the context of the Creation Sabbath, we must ask every pastor, priest, professor, pope and

Bible believer again—*Are you willing to abandon the seventh-day Sabbath of which Jesus said He is* LORD?

EVIDENCE #10. The Sabbath day is holy to the LORD.

Remember the Sabbath day to keep it holy. (Exodus 20:8)

Unbeknownst to the king, it was the last night of the Babylonian Empire. Nebuchadnezzar's grandson, King Belshazzar, had called a thousand of his cronies to a pleasure-driven banquet of revelry and drunkenness. In defiance of his grandfather's devotion to the God who created the heavens and the earth (Daniel 4:37), Belshazzar ordered this terrible sacrilege:

> **While he tasted the wine, Belshazzar gave the command to bring the gold and silver vessels which his father Nebuchadnezzar had taken from the temple which had been in Jerusalem, that the king and his lords, his wives, and his concubines might drink from them . . . And they drank wine, and praised the gods of gold and silver, bronze and iron, wood and stone.** (Daniel 5:2, 4)

The king now defiantly desecrated these sacred temple vessels, which had been consecrated to the worship of the LORD God Jehovah, and put them to illicit use. In short order, all of the eyes of the revelers were riveted upon the wall of the banquet hall as an unseen hand suddenly appeared, writing out Babylon's fate in words the King did not understand—*MENE , MENE, TEKEL, UPHARSIN* (Daniel 5:25). "Then the king's countenance changed, and his thoughts troubled him, so that the joints of his hips were loosed and his knees knocked against each other" (Daniel 5:6). At the king's mother's suggestion, Daniel, who was a captive from Judah and a veteran Babylonian statesman, was summoned to interpret the miraculous writing.

The words were addressed to the king. And what was their ominous meaning? " 'God has numbered your kingdom and finished it; . . . You have been weighed in the balance, and found wanting; . . .

Your kingdom has been divided, and given to the Medes and Persians' " (Daniel 5:26–28). At that very moment, the armies of Cyrus the Persian were in the process of ingeniously capturing the city of Babylon.

Belshazzar had breached protocol for that which is sacred. His pride and false sense of power made him insensitive to that which is holy. He had acted brashly and foolishly.

Years previous to the collapse of Babylon, the priests of Judah—the very ones who should have been devoted to explaining God's ways and instructing the multitudes in the worship of the Creator—were reproved for their failure to distinguish between that which is holy and that which is unholy. Through Ezekiel, God Himself identified their sin: " 'Her priests have violated my Law and profaned My holy things' " (Ezekiel 22:26). What was the most egregious issue of concern? The LORD God explained: " 'They have hidden their eyes from My Sabbaths, so that I am profaned among them.' " The priests of Judah had been commissioned to advance the spiritual sensibilities of the Israelite nation, but they were looking in the wrong direction. They had closed themselves to the plain evidence of Scripture and were in a state of self-deception. In doing so, they had disqualified themselves from their ordination as representatives of the Creator God and were culpable for the indifferent attitudes of the people toward this divine institution from Creation.

The Creator's words were unmistakable: " 'Remember the Sabbath day to keep it *holy* . . . the seventh day is the Sabbath of the LORD your God . . .' " (Exodus 20:8, emphasis supplied). Before the captivity, He had reiterated its sacredness as " 'My holy day' " (Isaiah 58:13) to be experienced in His honor. Across the entire world landscape, the seventh day in time is declared by the Creator God to be *holy* time—sacred time. It is a permanent weekly imprint in time because God is permanent in His love for humanity; and it is brought to worldwide attention with the most endearing of words—"remember."

In this connection, there are significant questions we must ask: *Why did God distinguish the seventh day of the week as "holy"? How can time be holy? What is it that humanity is privileged to experience in this weekly event? And what is it about the Sabbath's sacredness that God's enemy has tirelessly conspired to derail in the minds and hearts of humans?*

The answer to most of these questions can be found in the record of the origins of the human family—the Creation week (Genesis 1 and 2). It is there that the boundaries of nature and the parameters for humanity's well-being were established by the Creator.

In his article, "The Sabbath in the First Creation Account," professor of Old Testament studies and Dean of the Andrews University Theological Seminary, Jiri Moskala, summarized several features of the Creation week that bring surprising insight to the question of sacred time. **First,** he said:

Creation is a process of separation, division, and distinction. The word for 'separate' or 'distinct' is used five times in the Creation story itself (Genesis 1:4, 6, 7, 14, 18) . . . [these distinctions] reflect intentionality and design. God separated light from darkness, day from night, the heavens from the waters (sea), land from water, the Sabbath from the other six days.

So it is that, on the seventh day of Creation, God intentionally divided the time of the first six days from the holy time of the seventh. The fourth commandment expresses this as time for work and time for rest (Exodus 20:8).

Just as these physical distinctions remain in permanent reality today, so also does the original distinction between time and holy time. The seventh day (*Saturday*, in English speaking countries) is still *holy* time in our modern era.

Second, Dr. Moskala next described the Creation week of Genesis 1 as being "written in a beautiful literary structure that naturally falls into seven parts," corresponding to the seven days of the Creation. "The first, second, and third days are related to the *forming* activity of God. The fourth, fifth and sixth days are related to the *filling* activity of God. This literary structure demonstrates the beauty, balance, and unity of the biblical text." Professor Moskala concludes by noting the activity of *forming* and *filling:*

God first created space, and then He filled it with inhabitants. On the first day, God created light, and on the fourth day, He put lights or luminaries (Sun and Moon) in their place as 'inhabitants' of the light element. On the second day, He separated water from water by creating an expanse; and on the fifth day, filled the waters with fish and the sky with birds. On the third day, God formed dry land and the vegetation on it; and on the sixth day, He filled the land with the inhabitants He created—first a variety of land animals and creatures, and finally humans. He then gave humans and animals vegetation for food."

Dr. Moskala concluded by noting the distinct arrangement given to the seventh day:

As a final and climactic act of His creation, God made the seventh day—separating it from the other days of His creation and making it holy. Sabbath is a palace in time. God created/formed a very significant temporal space, but—much more than that—He also filled the time with His holiness. Thus, in the creation of the Sabbath, . . . forming and filling kiss each other. The Sabbath is the only day where forming and filling are put together.[28]

Other scholars have described the unique status of the seventh day. Nahum Sarna wrote that the Sabbath "as an institution is unparalleled in the ancient world."[29] Nichola Nigretti pointed out that, in the Creation story, the seventh day "concludes, brings to perfection and overcomes the preceding six days."[30] Regarding the strategic position of the seventh day, Gerhard Hasel reflected, "The conclusion of the Genesis Creation story indicates that just as man is the crown of Creation, so the seventh day, the Sabbath, is the final goal of Creation."[31]

And what is that goal? Why is God urging all humanity to experience this weekly sacred time? And why did Jesus announce that the Sabbath was made for mankind (Mark 2:27)? Dr. Moskala offered this insight:

The climax of the first Creation story is thus not the creation of humans but putting human beings in close intimate relationship with God! In other words, the culmination point of God's creative activity is not the sixth day (humans as a crown of God's physical creation), but the seventh-day Sabbath (humans in vivid mutual relationship with their holy Creator, worshiping Him). This climax teaches us that the Sabbath is the most important, not humans per se, but only humans in relationship with God; this is what counts. Sabbath is first of all about a relationship of beauty and splendor, of God with humans and humans with God.[32]

So, what is the result if a person should choose not to enter into this "palace" in time? Again, Dr. Moskala offered an answer: "In a palace the most important being is the king. But a king needs his people as much as the people need their king. In that sense, when we rupture our relationship with God, we break the Sabbath."

This background helps us to understand that the theme of Genesis 1 and 2 is "oneness"—oneness in family and oneness between human beings and God. The oneness began when God presented Eve to Adam and commanded our first parents to cling to each other, "and they shall become one flesh" (Genesis 2:24). This intimate relationship—holy matrimony, or marriage—forms the basis for the family unit.

Second, the seventh-day Sabbath was established to ensure the intimate union of the Creator with the human family. Humans, after all, were created in their Maker's image. This means that God can intimately relate to each human being in ongoing happiness and security. To know God is to love Him! Is this not the "oneness" that Jesus meant in His passionate prayer preceding His trial and crucifixion?

"And this is eternal life, that they may know You, the only true God, and Jesus Christ whom You have sent . . . that they all may be one, as You Father, are in Me, and I in You;

that they also may be one in Us, that the world may believe that You sent Me." (John 17:3, 21)

So it is an intimate "knowing" that God has designed for the sacred time of the seventh day. It is God's relational presence that makes the seventh day of weekly time sacred. It is Creation week and the Sabbath of the LORD that have provided humans in every age with God's answers to life's most formidable questions: *How did the human family originate? What is the purpose and meaning of life? And what is the destiny of the human family?* Is it any wonder that God's enemy has wished to unravel the meaning and purpose of the seventh-day Sabbath and cause it to appear as a discarded relic of the distant past?

The LORD challenged the priests of Judah to distinguish between the holy and unholy. He charged them with violating His Law and hiding their eyes from His Sabbaths. They had tarnished and unremembered the institution "unparalleled in the ancient world." Is there a renewed application of this reproof in modern times? How will today's God-fearing leaders respond?

As week by week the seventh day gently spreads its twenty-four hour palace of sacred time over the world, what will you choose? Will you allow the Word of God to obligate your conscience? Will you forge a new spiritual path that will bring God's promised presence and blessings into your life?

A nineteenth century author described the Sabbath as keeping company with Jesus. Dear reader, would you thoughtfully and prayerfully consider this invitation from the lips of Jesus given specifically to you?

"If you turn away your foot from the Sabbath, from doing your pleasure on My holy day, and call the Sabbath a delight, the holy day of the LORD honorable, and shall honor Him, not doing your own ways, nor finding your own pleasure, nor speaking your own words, then you shall delight yourself in the LORD; and I will cause you to ride on the high hills of the earth, and feed you with the heritage of Jacob your father. The mouth of the LORD has spoken." (Isaiah 58:13, 14)

To rise from error to truth is rare and beautiful.
—Victor Hugo

CHAPTER 12

"In-Flight" Course Correction

With the evidences for the Creation Sabbath fresh in mind, you may be asking: *Can this really be true? Why haven't I heard this before? How could I have missed understanding it like this? How could so many people be uninformed or misled for so many centuries?*

Others before us have discovered more missing truths in the story of the journey of Scripture through time. Truth seekers such as John Wycliffe, John Huss and his companion Jerome, Martin Luther, John Calvin, Savanarola, William Tyndale, John Knox and a host of others may have asked the same questions in their time. Their courage and their example can be our strength to walk through an opened spiritual door to embrace a new discovery about our LORD.

Yet the thrill of discovering Bible truth is contagious and rewarding. While it is always difficult for a person to re-examine long-cherished beliefs in determining whether his or her beliefs are true or not, this journey is noble and biblical. It is a rightful, joyful experience of growth in grace: "Examine yourselves as to whether you are in the faith. Prove yourselves" (2 Corinthians 13:5).

The Reformation drew its strength from the platform of believing that what God has said in Scripture must override all human ideology, philosophy and tradition. The Reformation's driving virtue was honesty with the Word of God and history. Its passion was the pursuit of the truth, both biblical and historical. These principles should prevail in every age.

We must ask: *Can any church or movement in Christianity continue to thrive without this formula? And can any person who has "put on Christ" be satisfied with anything less?*

In an appeal to readers to re-examine traditional beliefs, mid-twentieth-century Anglican rector of Holton, Somerset, England, Bernard L. Bateson, published the article, "Human Tradition or Biblical Truth?" In it he wrote:

> **During the course of the Church's history, times have come when the tradition of the centuries has had to be examined and set aside as unscriptural, despite its prevalence. Such was the case at the time of the Reformation, when many longstanding traditional teachings of the Church had to be swept away under the clear light of Bible truth . . .**

Bateson went on to record this warning:

> **But there has always been, on the other hand, a tendency to hold on to tradition at all costs, and a refusal to re-examine them afresh in light of the Bible.** (*Words of Life,* LXV, August 1961, p. 170; quoted in LeRoy Edwin Froom, *The Conditionalist Faith of Our Fathers,* vol. 2, p. 1013)

So, with the biblical and historical evidence at hand about the Saturday/Sunday question, we must ask: *Will the Christian world continue to let itself be held hostage by human ecclesiastical fiat? Is an "in-flight" course correction not possible for Christianity? Will individual Bible believers, who come to a knowledge of this crucial moral issue, have the courage of our spiritual forefathers who went before us?*

Does truth matter to you?

Is there a shortage of truth, absolute truth, in our world today—in the educational system, in the judicial system, in politics, in business, in the news? And what about the church?

Simply defined, truth is what is real. Truth is reality. It is what really is so. Jesus Himself identified the fountain of what is real when He said in His prayer: "Sanctify them by your truth. Your word is truth" (John 17:17). He was referring to all that God has revealed about Himself and His will for humanity through His prophets in Scripture.

Abraham Lincoln said, "History is not history unless it is the truth." Jesus announced, "I am the way, the *truth* and the life" (John 14:6, emphasis supplied). James Dobson reminded us, "It doesn't matter a whole lot what you and I think; what matters is what He [the Sovereign God] thinks."[33]

Is biblical truth merely decorative institutional trimming in the Christian worldview? Or is it rather a foundational treasure, a benchmark for all belief?

Theologian and professor R. C. Sproul has defined the value of truth in this way:

God is truth, and because truth is so intricately bound up with the very character of God, truth, all truth, is sacred. And when we transgress truth, we do violence to the author of truth, to God Himself. (*Renewing Your Mind* broadcast, March 19, 2004)

So what should I do when the Holy Spirit—"the Spirit of truth" (John 16:13)—reveals biblical reality to me?

The virtues of integrity, honesty and faithfulness are companions to truth, as the following vignette illustrates:

The merchant and the two tacks

Sarah Dillon had decided to surprise her eleven-year-old daughter Natilee with matching dresses, which she herself would make. Now she was watching patiently as the cloth she had selected was unwound onto the measuring table.

Owner of the small town mercantile store John Spencer began to measure out four yards for Sarah between the two tacks on the measuring table. One . . . two . . . three . . . four. Like his father and grandfather before him, John had measured thousands of yards for customers between those two thumbtacks.

When she arrived at home, Sarah excitedly began laying out the pattern for the dresses on the cloth. However, every way that she tried it, the pattern would not fit. The directions had called for four yards; yet, when Sarah used her yardstick to measure the cloth, it was short by several inches. Had John Spencer made a mistake?

Back at the store, Sarah explained her dilemma to John.

"It certainly is possible that I could have made a mistake," he said as he unfolded the material on the measuring table. With precision John began to re-measure Sarah's purchase between the two tacks. "There it is. I have given you four yards plus an inch. Will this satisfy you?"—he kindly asked.

Sarah was puzzled and somewhat embarrassed. "I'm confused, John. The pattern calls for four yards, and, try as I might, I couldn't get the pattern to fit within the amount of cloth you sold me." She hesitated and then daringly asked: "Are you certain the tacks are correct?"

John smiled and courteously answered with a sense of pride: "Sarah, I have been selling cloth over these tacks for years. My grandfather started this store fifty years ago. He and my father sold all their material between these two tacks."

There was a long pause before Sarah broke the silence: "Do you have a yardstick? For my satisfaction, would you be willing to measure the distance between the two tacks?"

John quickly agreed, he would readily uphold the reputation of his store. When he laid a yardstick beside the tacks, a look of shock came over his face. "It can't be possible! I can't understand it," he muttered. The tacks were nearly two inches shorter than the yardstick. It could not be denied. With a piercing look, he half-stuttered, "To think we have been selling cloth over those tacks for fifty years."

A moment of truth had come to the attention of John Spencer, owner of that small town store. For years he believed he had been giving an honest measure to every customer. He believed he was doing them right when actually—in ignorance—he was doing them wrong.

If John Spencer were to sell one more yard of cloth over those tacks, now that he knew, his conscience would convict him and his heart would condemn him.

What should he do? Without another moment slipping by, John reached into his pocket, took out his pocketknife, opened it and, with some effort, began prying up the tack out of its place. With the yardstick still laying on the counter, he placed the tack at the end and pressed it down with his thumb. Surprisingly, it went easily into the board. A closer look told him that the tack had gone into a previously existing hole that had been filled with putty. He had discovered the very hole from which the tack had been removed. At some point in time, someone had moved the tack! Someone was culpable for years of short-changing customers![34]

Yes, it is true—the LORD will not hold anyone accountable for that which they have not had an honest opportunity to know. "The times of this ignorance God winked at . . ." (Acts 17:30, KJV). Fortunately, it is our privilege to pursue His truth and to rejoice and embrace God's truth when it is made known to us. On the other hand, we are held to account for what we do know but to which we have declined to willingly respond.

A man blind from birth was healed by Jesus. Even with this evidence of Christ's divine nature, the on-looking Pharisees chose rather to be in denial and disbelief. With a touch of sarcasm, they asked Jesus: " 'Are we blind also?' Jesus said to them, 'If you were blind, you would have no sin; but now you say 'We see.' Therefore your sin remains' " (John 9:40, 41). To be sure, the world is now facing a moment of truth over sacred time. Catholics and Protestants of every shade of belief are facing this moment of truth. In the past, a "tack" has been surreptitiously moved out of its rightful place. Someone moved the "tack" and is culpable before God. The "tack" must be placed back in its original space. Must humanity continue to be short-changed of the promised blessing—the seventh-day blessing?

So it is that, through God's grace and providence, this moment of truth has come to you. Jesus' words of encouragement and warning are for all—" 'Walk while you have the light, lest darkness overtake you; he who walks in darkness does not know where he is going' " (John 12:35).

Now that you know the will of God for the seventh day, what will be your response? It is for you to decide!

*And I looked, and behold, a white cloud, and on the cloud sat One
like the Son of Man, having on His head a golden crown, and in His
hand a sharp sickle.* —John (Revelation 14:14)

CHAPTER 13

The Future of the Creation Sabbath

The book of Revelation, which is the "Revelation of Jesus Christ" (Revelation 1:1), is filled with hopeful promises. One of the most far-reaching of these is John's prediction: " 'And I saw a new heaven and a new earth, for the first heaven and the first earth had passed away' " (Revelation 21:1). The prediction goes on to describe God and redeemed humanity's dwelling together in God's restored social and physical order without death, sorrow, crying, or pain. This, of course, is a promise of the future that has stirred the heart and provided hope for believers the world over. The beauty and perfection of Eden will be restored!

The concept of "a new heaven and a new earth" did not originate in the book of Revelation. Like more than over four hundred other phrases and symbols in this apocalyptic letter from Jesus, the phrase is anchored in the Old Testament. The first exciting mention of "a new heaven and a new earth," as spoken by God Himself, is in the book of Isaiah:

"For as the new heaven and the new earth which I will make shall remain before Me," says the LORD, "so shall your descendants and your name remain. And it shall come to pass that from one New Moon to another [the endless cycle of time], and from one Sabbath to another, all flesh shall come to worship before Me," says the LORD. (Isaiah 66:22, 23)

Three features in this view of eternity, recorded by the gospel prophet Isaiah, relate directly to our subject:

First, when the LORD promised " 'your . . . name [shall] remain,' " it is a statement of permanent status for citizens in the courts of heaven. Unlike the lost who have forfeited their inheritance, those who have embraced redemption through the blood of Jesus are forever secure.

Second, the seventh-day Sabbath of Creation remains the ongoing centerpiece in God's relationship with the human race. " 'From one Sabbath to another' "—in unbroken cycle of time throughout eternity—God encircles His ransomed "jewels" with the blessing of His presence. The Sabbath day's permanent status—built into eternity—is God's assurance to the human race that they are forever in the embrace of their Maker. Their eternal home with God is secure.

Third, the weekly Sabbath in "the earth made new" is at the heart of universal *worship* of the Creator God. " 'All flesh shall come to worship before Me,' " God says. Redeemed humanity's constant worldview is one of awe, adoration and devotion to the Omnipotent God of love. This theme proclaimed by the redeemed—" 'Alleluia, Salvation and glory and honor and power to the LORD our God!' " (Revelation 19:1)—will never grow old.

In the earth made new, no one will be opting out for a Tuesday or a Thursday or a Sunday Sabbath. Just ask Him; He will remind you in person that it has always been the seventh day. In the earth made new, no one will be teaching that the seventh-day Sabbath is not important and doesn't matter anymore. Gathering on the Sabbath to worship God in adoration and thanksgiving will be heaven's most highly anticipated weekly attraction. Its theme will be *God is love!*

It is most significant that in promising an earth made new, God—the Monarch of the universe—has chosen to specifically identify the Sabbath of the fourth commandment as His appointment of deepest divine-human interaction—*worship!* Thus it was "in the beginning."

The theme of worship and the union of mind and heart with God dominates the landscape of Scripture. The divine order of worship—the sacred time of the seventh day, both at Creation in the beginning and in the future new earth to come—is God's handiwork.

The earth, in Genesis 1 and 2, began with the sanctifying and blessing of the seventh-day Sabbath—a blessing that would continue on. Jesus bridged the Sabbath into the New Testament era by announcing His lordship of the Sabbath and declaring that the Sabbath was made for humanity (Mark 2:27, 28). The "new earth" also begins with the declaration "from one Sabbath to another," and it continues throughout eternity. From Scripture the Creator God has assuredly made His divine order of "sacred time" plain and documented.

The theme of continuity and uninterrupted progression of the Creation Sabbath conveys to the human family the faithfulness of the Creator God. Sacred time—the seventh day—is the bedrock of God's relationship with humanity. By it He tells us, "I love you! I will never forsake you!"

Professor Terence Fretheim of Luther Seminary referred to this as the "created order of things" and that departing from it is to bring this aspect of Creation to "chaos." Here are his words:

The sabbath is thus a divinely given means for all creatures to be in tune with the created order of things. Even more, *sabbath-keeping is an act of creation-keeping*. To keep the sabbath is to participate in God's intention for the rhythm of creation. Not keeping the sabbath is a violation of the created order; it returns one aspect of that order to chaos. What the creatures do with the sabbath has cosmic effects. (*Exodus,* John Knox Press, Louisville, 1991, p. 230, emphasis in original)

Human attempts to alter, suppress or abandon the Creation Sabbath can now be understood as a breach of the divine order. Yet, is it given to humans to out-think their Maker?

On account of this biblical perspective, we must raise the question with every believer, whether pastor, priest, professor, pope or Bible student: *Why?—why has Christianity for nearly two thousand years allowed the disruption of the divine order of sacred time spoken of in the fourth commandment—the very centerpiece of the worship of the true and only Creator God?*

As a result of this centuries old displacement, is it not true that a first class treasure has been lost to many generations and that Christianity, and ultimately, humanity are less than they were meant to be?

Deeper issues in the Saturday/Sunday conflict

It is because of this reality—a major human disruption in the divine order of sacred time—that the conflict over Saturday and Sunday should be understood. Indeed! It is more than an issue of which day.

The spirit of disruption originated in heaven itself—"And war broke out in heaven: . . . the great dragon was cast out, that serpent of old, called the Devil and Satan, who deceives the whole world; he was cast to the earth, and his angels were cast out with him" (Revelation 12:7, 9).

A psychotic liar is on the loose. His aim is to disrupt God's order for humanity, distort reality, and wage a campaign to smear God's character, discredit His reputation, and demoralize the planet in the name of "freedom." His craft is to never appear as he really is but to work under the subterfuge of human agencies. His strategy is to recast that which is morally right as being rigid, restrictive and arbitrary. That which is morally wrong is crafted as being exhilarating, progressive and liberating. Every successful scheme to substitute his will in the place of God's will is an evil satisfaction to his narcissistic ego. On every occasion that humans succumb to his will, they unwittingly pay homage to his rebellion.

The telltale trademark of false worship

So, it is not surprising that the primary issue that will bring earth's history to a close—worship—is first brought into view in the original family on earth. The sons of Adam and Eve—Cain and Abel—came to *worship* before the LORD (Genesis 4). God accepted the prescribed offering of worship brought in faith by Abel—the blood of a slain lamb representing the good news of grace that God had provided a Savior from sin for humans.

But Cain proposed to alter the worship of the Creator God, offering the fruit of his own efforts and devising. Rather than take God at His word, Cain's choice represents all human inventions that are meant to fulfill the desire for worship but fall short of God's prescription. Self-serving as they are, they represent human attempts to bring substitutes in the place of the real thing—a heartfelt acknowledgment of the Creator God that is shown in taking God at His word.

However earnest and wholehearted Cain may have appeared, for God to accept Cain's alternate offering would be to approve of a mischaracterization of the plan of salvation—that the sinner is accepted and saved on the basis of human effort. Cain had deliberately brought an offering that took the place of what God had prescribed. But it was a disruption in the divine order.

In effect, Cain had made himself the judge; he had placed his judgment over that of his Maker. And this is the telltale trademark upon which all false worship rests. This is the spirit of disruption.

Centuries later, the covenant nation of Israel habitually chose alternative gods to serve—a perversion of divine worship known as idolatry. God regretfully summarized her repeated choice: " '. . . you have forgotten Me and trusted in falsehood' " (Jeremiah 13:25). Since the LORD considered Himself Israel's husband (Isaiah 54:5, 6), He spoke of her forgetfulness and waywardness in the strongest social terms, yet in terms that appropriately describe the disruption of the divine order—" 'I have seen your *adulteries* and your *lustful neighings*, the lewdness of your *harlotry*, your *abominations* on the hills in the fields. Woe to you, O Jerusalem! Will you still not be made clean?' " (Jeremiah 13:27, emphasis supplied)

Jesus and His face-off with the disruptor

So it was that the Son of God was brought to the same issue as that of Cain and Abel, of Israel, and, really, of all humanity—Who is worthy to be worshiped?

Robing himself in the disguise of an angel of light—a likeness of his former appearance—Satan deftly approached Jesus, weakened after forty days without food. With the mission of Jesus in view to rescue this lost world from its plight, the usurper proposed a substitute plan:

Again, the devil took Him up on an exceedingly high mountain, and showed Him all the kingdoms of the world

134

and their glory. And he said to Him, "All these things I will give You if You will fall down and worship me." (Matthew 4:8, 9)

Christ's adversary, who now was tempting Him, had made himself the foremost disruptor of the divine order. He was an angelic being chronically self-inflicted with rebellion. Now the deceiver was offering Jesus a shortcut, a bloodless alternative for the plan to rescue the planet. Would Jesus spare Himself of the spilling of His life-blood to save humanity from sin? Would He abandon the shame, anguish and humiliation of the cross, which is the full expression of God's love and grace for a fallen world? And would He succumb to the temptation to fall down and worship the originator of disruption? In reality, Jesus was being tempted with the supreme falsehood of all falsehoods concocted by the father of lies (John 8:44)—no created being is ever worthy of worship.

It should surprise no one that Satan would make such a proposal. He has an insatiable lust to be worshiped, an unending need to authenticate his quest to outstrip and out-flank his Maker. Lurking in the shadows, he stands behind every human attempt to alter the divine order. His craving is for worship, and every deviation from the divine order of the Creator that he can inspire humans to adopt is homage they unwittingly give to this usurper. In this way he summarily mocks God continuously.

For this reason, it is Satan's studied occupation to entice human participation in his scenario of falsehoods. And, yes, it is even within his scope to create a human system that has an appearance of Christianity that really is not Christianity.

He has already succeeded once before in doing this to the Jewish system of religion. And what is the evidence for this? When Jesus arrived in Israel, no one expected a suffering Messiah as predicted in Isaiah 53. John the Baptist's appeal at the Jordan River for repentance was an ancient idea that had been forgotten. He rightfully labeled the Pharisees and Sadducees, who came to the Jordan to hear him, a "brood of vipers" (Matthew 3:7), for they had twisted the Old Testament teachings for their own purposes. When John announced Jesus as the "lamb of God," not even Jesus' disciples associated their

Master as the reality of the blood offering of the sacrificial lamb at the temple. God's glorious temple itself had been turned into a "den of thieves" (Matthew 21:13). Then, when the chief priests and scribes saw the wonderful things Jesus was doing, "they were indignant" (Matthew 21:15). The cry of the crowd, "Crucify Him!" was the result of the rabid efforts of the father of falsehoods. This was the disoriented condition of a once-flourishing Israelite faith.

Christ's answer to Satan's insidious proposal was swift and direct—a safeguard for all of His followers throughout time:

Then Jesus said to him, "Away with you, Satan! For it is written, 'You shall worship the LORD** your God, and Him only you shall serve.' "** (Matthew 4:10)

In this, Jesus cited Old Testament Scripture (Deuteronomy 6:13; Exodus 34:14). He knew that there are no shortcuts and no legitimate substitutes and that the only safe course is to take God at His word.

After being shown the kingdoms of the world, Jesus' last temptation was about worship. It was the temptation that was broadest in scope. Once again we are able to sense that the pivotal issue before all humanity in every age is that of *worship*. And the fourth commandment is at the very heart of this conflict.

An appearance of Christianity documented

So, it should not take the thoughtful student of Bible prophecy, church history and current events by surprise to expect Christ's enemy to engineer the rise of an appearance of Christianity that is not real Christianity. We might also suspect that in such a system this deceiver would bring about an appearance of worship that is a counterfeit of the genuine. Counterfeits work best when they are close to the true.

What are the evidences that such a system did come into being and still exists? We have already documented the essential history of such an alteration of worship. But what does Jesus Himself reveal and warn about this ominous and daring course in history?

The first hint in the New Testament is from the Apostle Paul as he warned his fellow believers in Ephesus in a farewell address:

"I have not shunned to declare to you the whole counsel of God. . . . For I know this, that after my departure savage wolves will come in among you, not sparing the flock. Also from among yourselves men will rise up, speaking perverse things, to draw away the disciples after themselves. Therefore watch, and remember that for three years I did not cease to warn everyone night and day with tears." (Acts 20:27–31)

Under inspiration of the Holy Spirit, Paul labeled this rise of an apparent Christianity as "the lawless one" (2 Thessalonians 2:8). He also described it as the "son of perdition [destruction], who opposes and exalts himself above all that is called God or that is worshiped, so that he sits as God in the temple of God, showing himself that he is God" (2 Thessalonians 2:3, 4).

Paul did not view this as happening scores of centuries into the future, but he said "the mystery of iniquity is already at work . . ." (verse 7).

While the making of an apparent system of Christianity is that of human devising, Paul identified the underlying intelligence behind this early development in Christianity: "The coming of the lawless one is according to the working of Satan, with all power, signs, and lying wonders, and with all unrighteous deception . . ." (verse 9, 10).

What does it take for a person to be fortified against this consuming force of falsehood supported by miracles? Paul's answer is: "the love of the truth" (verse 10). Without this chosen state of mind and heart and without the Scriptures as a truth detector, Paul declared that God will allow a person to become deluded "that they should believe the lie" (verse 11).

Now we are ready to understand what Jesus has revealed. The book of Revelation was authored by Jesus; John the apostle is His penman. Christ's messages in Revelation propose to show "things which must shortly take place" (Revelation 1:1). The imagery, symbols, descriptions and events are meant to be a blessing, a safeguard and encouragement to the person who is willing to "hear" and "keep" what is revealed (Revelation 1:3).

A record of spiritual battle

Revelation portrays in colorful symbolic style the spiritual battle between good and evil from the time of the first outbreak of rebellion in heaven until the eventual destruction of sin and the earth made new. It is a forecast of the play and counterplay between Jesus and Satan. Humans are the actors who choose between truth and falsehood.

Revelation tells the story of Satan's attempt to destroy Christ's church by discrediting and eradicating it with the same vengeance that he used in attempting to annihilate Jesus. "And the dragon [Satan] was enraged . . . and went to make war . . ." (Revelation 12:17).

Thus, the book of Revelation is about how the peoples of the world throughout time respond to the great epic event of all human history—the crucifixion and resurrection of Jesus Christ. In addition, the question that every person must answer is: *Will I approach the Scriptures with a desire to conform to the will of God?*

In the book of Revelation, Jesus gave John the symbols of two women. Drawing from imagery in the Old Testament, where a woman represents God's people (Jeremiah 6:2) and from the New Testament, where His church is His bride (2 Corinthians 11:2), Jesus represents two kinds of Christianity—one that faithfully upholds His Word and another that unfaithfully confuses His Word.

The first woman represented is in Revelation 12:1, 2. She is virtuous and faithful and is "clothed with the sun, and with the moon under her feet, and on her head a garland of twelve stars." The Child to whom she gave birth "was to rule all nations with a rod of iron. And her Child was caught up to God and to His throne" (verse 5). Pursued by the dragon for eradication, the woman was lifted to the safety of the wilderness on eagles' wings and providentially spared. Both she and her offspring are identified as those "who keep the commandments of God and have the testimony of Jesus" (Revelation 12:17).

The harlot of Revelation

The second woman, described by Jesus and given by the angel to John, sits on a "scarlet beast which was full of names of blasphemy,

138

having seven heads and ten horns" (Revelation 17:3). The kings of the earth have become infatuated with her and commit fornication with her; also, "the inhabitants of the earth were made drunk with the wine of her fornication" (verse 2). The intoxicating "wine" that she offers is the false teachings and mischaracterizations that blaspheme and undermine God.

This is the symbolic scene as written by John:

The woman was arrayed in purple and scarlet, and adorned with gold and precious stones and pearls, having in her hand a golden cup full of abominations and the filthiness of her fornication. (Revelation 17:4)

One feature of this system, which has an appearance of Christianity, struck a troubling mood of great consternation for the Apostle John. This is what he discovered:

And I saw the woman, drunk with the blood of the saints and with the blood of the martyrs of Jesus. And when I saw her, I marveled with great amazement. (Revelation 17:6)

These features summarize the second woman of Revelation. Her renown is worldwide; she courts political favor with nations; her falsehoods bring a drunken stupor. Her strategy is to quiet the opposition by force; her name is "Babylon" because she has mixed with Christianity practices foreign to Christianity, resulting in doctrinal confusion (Revelation 17:5); she claims to be above God's law and is known as the "lawless one." Her daughters resemble her; the archenemy of Jesus expands her influence through miracles and lying wonders.

As we shall see, it is the "beast"—a long-standing religious-political system—upon which the woman sits. It is this system that will daringly take center stage in a climactic showdown with the Creator over worship (Revelation 13).

Stacking up the evidence

Jesus was an insightful expositor of prophecy. He referenced the prophet Daniel when He predicted the coming destruction of Jerusalem (Matthew 24:15). On one occasion He told His disciples, " 'I still have many things to say to you, but you cannot bear them now' " (John 16:12).

Bible expositors throughout the centuries have often pointed out parallel descriptions between the unfolding prophecies of Daniel and those of the book of Revelation. In fact, Daniel was told that his book would shine brightest in application at the "time of the end" (Daniel 12:9). His book is a platform for understanding the spiritual issues that dominate the time of the end. It identifies the same system as does Revelation in the appearance of Christianity that is not real Christianity.

God is quite candid in alerting the wise about developments in the battle between His kingdom of grace and the kingdom of darkness. He does this so that people who really want to know can be open-eyed about what is going on in the flow of events. He really wants all to be aware of the issues so they will not be taken by surprise and so they can make good choices as a result.

The prophet Daniel was especially disturbed about the symbolic portrayal of the little horn, which forced its way among ten previously existing horns on the head of the grotesque and terribly dreadful fourth beast in his vision (Daniel 7:7, 8). An angel explained to Daniel that he was seeing the unfolding of world empires and that the fourth beast would eventually collapse, giving rise to other lesser powers. Comparing Daniel 7 with Daniel 8, we recognize that this dreadful fourth beast represents the powerful and ruthless Roman Empire. The little horn that emerged from the fourth beast had "eyes like the eyes of a man, and a mouth speaking pompous [blasphemous] words" (Daniel 7:8).

The incredible news about the little horn's pompous words so shocked Daniel that he became emotionally troubled (Daniel 7:15). Knowing that the God of Israel was the object of its blasphemous attack caused him deep concern, spurring him to ask about this future development. This is how the vision's attending host explained the particulars of the little horn:

The ten horns are ten kings who shall arise from this kingdom. And another shall rise after them; he shall be different from the first ones, and shall subdue three kings. He shall speak pompous words against the Most High, shall persecute the saints of the Most High, *and shall intend to change times and law.* Then the saints will be given into his hand for a time and times and half a time. (Daniel 7:24, 25, emphasis supplied)

Besides being a prophet, Daniel was also a statesman for two empires—Babylon and Medo-Persia. What he saw revealed in vision greatly perplexed him, so much so that it was reflected in his countenance. To this governor of empires, this was a serious, grievous development toward the God of Israel and His future followers.

The little horn's attempt to "change times and law" and its claim to have religious authority even to blaspheme God, suggests that the little horn would attempt to alter a law of God relating to time. From the historical study that has already been presented, we have seen that the seventh day of the fourth commandment is that law of God that has to do with sacred time. It is this law that the little horn attempted to change. As we have already seen, papal Rome candidly acknowledges exchanging Sunday for the Sabbath, a historical fulfillment of Daniel 7:25.

The little horn's attempt to alter the time stated in the fourth commandment is a devious assault on God's authority, disrupting the sacred time for the worship of the Creator God—the seventh day.

Worship is the fundamental issue that repetitively shows up in the book of Daniel—humanly mandated worship in substitution for God's order of worship. It is a repeat of the attitude of Cain who unwisely and daringly chose to substitute his judgment for that of his Maker. With the alteration made by the papacy, the issue of worship is much larger and more far-reaching in time. The attending host in Daniel's vision regarded this assault on a divine institution as blaspheming God.

That God would predict a serious disruption of sacred time before it happened assures us of three things: (1) the Word of God can be trusted; (2) the Creator God never intended for the seventh-day

Sabbath to be altered; (3) the instituting of an alternate day in place of the seventh day is an intentional assault on God's authority and veracity. Heaven considers it blasphemous because it represents human action assuming to do what is only God's prerogative to do.

From the twenty-first century vantage point, we are able to look back over history and see that what God predicted through Daniel—who lived over five hundred years before Christ—really has happened. And we are living in its aftermath.

Daniel's forecast of earth's final issue

Remarkably, the book of Daniel describes three major stories in which the primary issue is *worship*. Two of these stories feature human inventions of worship that placed God's servants in a serious dilemma.

Story one. The incident happens on the plain of Dura, where three brave men stand tall while all others, by the king's command, are bowing before a colossal image. Officials of Babylon charge the three men—Shadrach, Meshach, and Abed-Nego, who happen to be Daniel's companions—before King Nebuchadnezzar: "They do not serve your gods or worship the gold image which you have set up" (Daniel 3:12). The king had decreed a death penalty—anyone who dared to not bend the knee before the golden image that the king has erected was to be burned alive in the fiery furnace. Thrown into the furnace as their punishment, the three Hebrews stand miraculously unscathed in the roaring fire, accompanied by a fourth person who is the Son of God (Daniel 3:25). King Nebuchadnezzar is amazed and confesses the superiority of the Hebrew God who delivered them.

Story two. Prideful King Nebuchadnezzar, intoxicated with an exaggerated sense of self-importance, is stripped of his reason and caused to roam as a wild beast for seven years (Daniel 4:25). When his sense of rationality returns to him—and he is humbled and able to understand himself—the king wonderfully acknowledges the God of heaven and earth and is able to declare in worship: "Now I, Nebuchadnezzar, praise and extol and honor the King of heaven, all of whose works are truth, and His ways justice. And those who walk in pride He is able to abase" (Daniel 4:37).

Story three. Transferred to the Medo-Persian Empire after the fall of Babylon, Daniel counsels King Darius as a trusted counselor and governor. His excellent spirit and judicious advice distinguish Daniel above the other governors.

Jealous over his faultless record of service, these officials in the king's inner circle conspire to trap Daniel in his open worship of the Creator God. With his window open toward Jerusalem, Daniel can be seen in prayer three times a day.

Under the pretense of showing honor to the king, these conspirators make the king a proposal: "All the governors of the kingdom, the administrators and satraps, the counselors and advisers, have consulted together to establish a royal statute and to make a firm decree, that whoever petitions any god or man for thirty days, except you, O king, shall be cast into the den of lions" (Daniel 6:7).

Unaware of their scheme, the king signs the decree. Though Daniel is aware of the new law, he does not flinch in his continued practice of approaching God in prayer and worship. Giddily, the jealous government officials report his violation of the law. When the king finds out the real purpose of the law, he becomes "greatly displeased with himself" (verse 14) and attempts to spare Daniel from the lion's den. Sadly, he recognizes that the decree cannot be reversed.

Honoring Daniel—and his God—the king declares, "Your God, whom you serve continually, He will deliver you" (verse 16). Daniel is thrown to the lions, and the king spends a troubling night without eating or sleeping. The next day, the king is overjoyed to discover that God has spared Daniel. The hungry lions' mouths have been miraculously shut. The conspiracy has been turned on its head.

The book of Daniel is a harbinger of the "time of the end" (Daniel 12:4). It teaches those living in the final hours of earth's history that the issue of *worship* will be the world's concluding test. Story one and three strategically show that false worship is of human devising and that its perpetrators need the threat of state-sponsored force—even death decrees—to get people to comply.

Is there a counterpart to these stories in the book of Revelation? And will there be a re-match over *worship,* though on a worldwide scale? Will that re-match also include a state-sponsored death decree as the way to enforce it?

The "little horn" comes to Revelation

The Apostle John describes in Revelation's thirteenth chapter what he next saw in vision—an uncanny likeness to the "little horn" of Daniel 7:25. In Revelation 13, the symbolism has changed from four distinct beasts into a single seven-headed beast (Revelation 13:1)—the same beast that carries Revelation's purple and scarlet-robed woman (Revelation 17:1–5). In both Daniel and Revelation, beasts are symbolic of political systems. They are usually superpowers in their time.

Notice the beast's distinguishing features: (1) he has a mouth speaking "great things and blasphemies . . . against God" (Revelation 13:5, 6); (2) his power extends over forty-two months—which is the equivalent of 1260 prophetic years (verse 5); (3) he makes war upon the saints to crush them (verse 7).

Jesus, through His angel, gives the Apostle John these additional details: in its history, one of the beast's heads is to be given a mortal wound that will later be healed (verse 3) and the authority that this head claims extends to every tribe, tongue and nation (verse 7). Yet, this "authority," according to the prophecy, is not derived from Jesus nor the Holy Spirit but from "the dragon [who] gave him his power, his throne, and great authority" (verse 2). This is the "little horn" of Daniel 7 with an expanded resume. It is the same system, a pontificate system, that has the appearance of Christianity. Moreover, as described in Daniel 7, it thinks to change God's law that distinguishes sacred time—the seventh day.

The future predicted

Revelation 13 sets the stage for the concluding events that occur before the second coming of Jesus Christ. The players are all identified; the component powers are in place. However, the fuse of tumultuous world events that ignites the powder keg still remains hidden from the prophetic horizon. Revelation 13 describes what will occur once it is lit.

Five times Revelation 13 mentions "worship." Surprisingly, none of these mentions are with reference to God. Each time it is worship that is focused on the seven-headed beast. These are a prediction of the final issue that will engulf the entire world—*worship*.

We must remember that the adulterous woman who rides the beast has already made the world drunk with the wine of her fornication. This is the system of false teachings that gives the appearance of Christianity while actually mischaracterizing the Creator God. One of these mischaracterizations has to do with the "time" of *worship*. And, yes, you may have already guessed it from the documentation of this book, it is a disruption of the divine order, an alternate *time* of worship determined by man and not God.

Considering the context of Revelation 13, we can see that the issue of Saturday versus Sunday is more than a matter of which particular day a Christian worships. Rather, the issue is: *To whom will each person living on earth give homage and show loyalty? Will it be to the beast system, or will it be to the Creator God? In the end, to whom will a person choose to obligate his conscience?* Here is Revelation's prediction:

And all who dwell on the earth will worship him, whose names have not been written in the Book of Life of the Lamb slain from the foundation of the world. (Revelation 13:8)

This is a serious development. Is this the global event toward which the worship stories of the book of Daniel portend? Will the populations of the world choose a worship that is promoted by miraculous signs and fire coming out of the sky (Revelation 13:13), or will it be the worship of the Creator according to God's specified design? Will it be a human alteration such as Cain devised, or will it be that which is specified by the LORD Himself?

The second beast of Revelation 13

In solemn description, the last half of Revelation 13 describes a second beast whose origin is out of the earth rather than from the sea. It constructs an image—a modern restoration of the beast-system in a religious-political system that needs the state to enforce its dogma—to advance the worship brought into acceptance by the seven-headed beast. In its rise to prominence, the second beast at first speaks like a lamb but later speaks like a dragon. By miraculous wonders and "great signs" the populations of the earth will be deceived (verses 12–14).

And, yes, for anyone who has read Revelation 13, there is the telltale mark of all false worship that we noted in the book of Daniel—a state-sponsoring power to enforce that worship!

He was granted power to give breath to the image of the beast, that the image of the beast should both speak and cause as many as would not worship the image of the beast to be killed. (verse 15).

We must remember that this worldwide move to give homage to the beast's system of worship is in the context of a severe "time of trouble"—it is the worst that this world will have ever experienced (Daniel 12:1). Why this will happen should come as no surprise: A loud voice from heaven says: ". . . Woe to the inhabitants of the earth and of the sea! For the devil has come down to you, having great wrath, because he knows that he has a short time" (Revelation 12:12).

Satan will pull out all the weapons of deception in his arsenal. It will take place in a final scenario of desperation after Satan's long history of marshaling the populations of the world against the Creator. He works through human agents, one of which John described in Revelation: "He performs great signs, so that he even makes fire come down from heaven on the earth in the sight of men. And he deceives those who dwell on the earth by those signs which he was granted to do in the sight of the beast . . ." (Revelation 13:13, 14).

Will anyone be spared from this barrage of miracles and lying wonders, which are meant to authenticate the beast's system of worship? Is there a way to be protected against the supernatural appearances that will captivate the unprepared? Yes, if a person has come to distrust his senses—what he sees, hears and feels—and to trust only what the Scriptures reveal. The truth of the Bible is our only safeguard.✳

What do the Scriptures reveal?

We are left to ask: What it is that will cause the second beast of Revelation 13 to bring the world to this moment of decision under a death decree? What is it that will arouse God's enemy to pull out all the stops? Why will Satan's fury turn to miraculous acts of desperation to mislead and deceive people all over the world?

While the great schoolrooms of the world promote secularism and atheism and act as if there is no God, Satan well knows that there is! Wrote James: "Even the demons believe—and tremble!" (James 2:19). Satan is also a master at understanding Bible prophecy—even to the point of leading humans to invent false prophetic interpretations to mask the real anti-Christ of Daniel 7 and Revelation 13 and confuse students of Bible prophecy about the second coming of Christ.

So, the prophecy that disturbs Satan and arouses his indignation the most is the one that he heard from the lips of Jesus:

And this gospel of the kingdom will be preached in all the world as a witness to all nations, and then the end will come. (Matthew 24:14)

In the chapter immediately following Revelation 13, Jesus amplifies the prophecy of Matthew 24 in response to Satan's intensified efforts to deceive the world, using an array of lying wonders, miracles and, eventually, fire from the sky. The amplified message begins as follows:

Then I saw another angel flying in the midst of heaven, having the everlasting gospel to preach to those who dwell on the earth—to every nation, tribe, tongue, and people— saying with a loud voice, "Fear God and give glory to Him, for the hour of His judgment has come; and *worship Him who made heaven and earth, the sea and springs of water.*" (Revelation 14:6, 7, emphasis supplied)

This is an angelic message—an appeal coming right out of the courts of heaven. It is loud, persistent, and universal. The Creator God has purposed that, before the end, every person must be alerted to the reality of the true character and love of God for humanity. The "everlasting gospel" is the salvation story centered in the life, crucifixion and resurrection of Jesus Christ. It is heaven's climactic appeal that every person may acknowledge God and receive His mercy and grace and enter into a saving relationship with their Maker.

You may have already concluded correctly that Revelation 14 is the antitheses of Revelation 13. These are two strategic opposing propositions. In these two chapters we are taken back to the beginning—to the altars of Cain and Abel. When the prophecy is fulfilled, the populations of the world will metaphorically choose at which altar they will worship.

The theme of both chapters is "worship." The worship of Revelation 13 is that which is promoted by the seven-headed beast. The worship of Revelation 14 is that which is enjoined by the One who "made heaven and earth, the sea and the springs of water." The first worship is under the authority of the dragon; the second has the authority and divine credentials that come from the very throne of God.

So, indeed, it can now be understood that the issue of worship really is deeper than that of Saturday versus Sunday. It is an issue of loyalty, integrity and fidelity to the Creator God. This is the final spiritual showdown in the long conflict between the Creator God and a rebel angel. During this time, the Creator of heaven and earth is giving His final appeal to the earth's inhabitants:

Fear God and give glory to Him for the hour of His judgment has come, and worship Him who made heaven and earth, the sea and the springs of water. (Revelation 14:7)

This worship is the exact opposite of that which is promoted by the seven-headed beast of Revelation 13. Those who fear God and give Him glory are called to worship that is rooted in the fourth commandment. The angelic message of Revelation 14:6, 7 uses the very words of the Sabbath commandment—"**. . . made the heavens and the earth, the sea . . .**" (Exodus 20:11). Here are repeated the veritable words of the Creator God during the "time of the end," calling the world's inhabitants back to the "original LORD's day." Those who fear God and realize the solemnity of God's judgment hour will respond affirmatively.

Examine the text more closely. Significantly, we find the three basic elements of a sovereign's seal (such as that of the president of the United States) also present in the fourth commandment:

Name: **"God"**
Title: **"made"** (Creator)
Domain: **"heaven and the earth, the sea"**

Revelation's good news about Babylon

A dramatic scene now unfolds in Revelation 18:1. Here another angelic messenger from heaven appears. His message is both a flashback and an addition to the messages of the angels of Revelation 14. The new angel descends with "great authority, and the earth was illuminated with his glory." This is a tell-all message about Babylon's reputation and spiritual condition. It is a bleak and revealing exposé. For the sake of earth's inhabitants, Heaven must provide the evidence of Babylon's true condition and warn the world of her imminent fate:

> **And he cried mightily with a loud voice saying, "Babylon the great is fallen, is fallen, and has become the habitation of demons, a prison for every foul spirit, and cage for every unclean and hated bird!"** (Revelation 18:2, 3)

In response to this announcement, John hears another voice. This time it is a voice that comes directly from the court of heaven itself. Whose voice is it? Is it not the voice of Jesus, urgently speaking to His people throughout the world? You decide!

> **And I heard another voice from heaven saying, "Come out of her, *my people*, lest you share in her sins, and lest you receive of her plagues. For her sins have reached to heaven,**

and God has remembered her iniquities." (Revelation 18:4, 5, emphasis supplied)

Ironically, there is amazingly good news here! While Babylon, through the centuries of her existence, has made the world "drunk with the wine of her fornication" (false teachings that mischaracterize God), Jesus has people in the midst of Babylon who are honest in heart and are earnestly and sincerely following Him to the extent of their knowledge. These are accepted of Him. When additional evidence and added understanding of Scripture is shown to them, they have a mind to embrace it. And now Jesus speaks this urgent imperative to them: **"Come out of her, *my people*!"**

This is a command with promise! It is an urgent warning like that of a loving father, crying out to his children who are about to be swallowed by a raging fire of which they are unaware. In this case, mystical Babylon has fallen and is about to meet her fiery end (Revelation 18:5–24).

These angelic messages found in Revelation 14 and 18 are for contemporary humanity. We live in the time of the end! These messages—and the fact that you are now aware of them—are meant to be the voice of God to your soul. If you are serious about taking God at His word, this is the lens through which you may read the unfolding of world events leading to the second coming of Jesus. Your voice, sharing with others the reality of these heavenly messages, will add to the groundswell of intensity that God has predicted.

Expanding the worship of the Creator God

We have now seen that heavenly agencies have entered the events of the "time of the end" to urgently appeal for people to fear God and worship Him who created our planet. This urgent message comes right out of God's Written Word. It is meant for all peoples, including those who have been held hostage by the "spiritual empire" that invented the human disruption of God's divine order of "sacred time."

There are many today who are hungering for the light of God's Word to shine upon them. Many are questioning the meaning of the progression of world events and are seeking to understand the issues

150

of this complex, unsettled era. Millions of people need to be prepared to meet their Creator upon His arrival to deliver His people from the darkness of the earth (Daniel 12:1, 2).

The evidences for the Creation Sabbath are intellectually and emotionally compelling. The Sabbath's centuries old exile—in the cobwebbed halls of forgetfulness—is over. The Sabbath day is God made, biblically founded, and Christ exalting. It amazingly unifies people who love to be in the holy presence of Jesus; it has no ethnic, economic or national boundaries, and its blessing is lavishly rained upon all who will embrace it.

For these reasons, it is imperative that Catholics and Protestants be in the forefront of advancing the recovery of the original LORD's day. The LORD will prepare the way for an amazing surge in the spread of this truth to the four corners of the earth. God-fearing pastors, professors, priests and Bible believers everywhere must take the lead—for the sake and honor of the Creator God—to herald the lost meaning, delight and divine blessing of the seventh day of Scripture and of Jesus Christ. (For expositions from two leading Evangelicals urging seventh-day Sabbath observance, see Supporting Exhibit #1, on page 158.)

A quick response from Catholics and Protestants

No one can outwit the Creator God. This is His hour to outmatch and outmaneuver the enemy, whose time is short (Revelation 12:12). So what are the factors that will turn many to embrace the gospel message of Revelation 14:6, 7? And why will Sunday-observing Catholic and Protestant followers of Jesus everywhere under conviction move decisively to embrace the worship of the Creator God over the worship of the beast system of Revelation 13?

The primary factor is the outpouring of the Holy Spirit as on the Day of Pentecost, recorded in the book of Acts, chapter 2. The prophet Joel predicted this urgent moving upon the world's populations just before the return of Jesus:

And it shall come to pass afterward that I will pour out My Spirit upon all flesh; . . . Before the great and terrible [awesome] day of the LORD. And it shall come to pass that who-

ever calls on the name of the L<small>ORD</small> shall be saved. . . . (Joel 2:28, 31, 32)

This text is synonymous with the description in Revelation 18:1:

After these things I saw another angel coming down from heaven, having great authority, and the earth [the entire world] was illuminated with his glory.

Under the roar of spiritual confusion and the distractions of this world, the joyous result will be that multitudes from all nations will, with gratitude, respond to the imperative to "worship Him who made heaven and earth, the sea and springs of water."

This is the angelic message that lit the fire of devotion for Joseph Bates and for thousands who would follow. It is the message that has called millions worldwide to embrace the gospel within the context of Jesus Christ's Creation Sabbath.

The world is becoming ripe for God's harvest. Today there are many contemporary, honest-hearted, God-fearing followers of Jesus Christ who are committed to the sovereignty of God's Word.

And now God's appeal has come to you in the pages of this book. You are standing at the point of decision where Adam and Eve, in the beginning, once stood—*Will you be willing to take God at His word?*

The Creator God is worthy of your worship! He is worthy for your stepping forward eagerly to follow. It was for *you* that Jesus Christ in Gethsemane chose to go to Golgotha's cross. It is *you* that He wishes to have at His side in eternity. It is not happenstance that you have come to a fuller awareness of His will for you. If this is your heart's desire, you may live your life with His assurance.

The parable of the king's ten sons

The king of a vast empire had ten sons of whom he was very proud. They were each a reflection of the king's poise, wisdom and character. Prior to leaving on an extended journey, the king gathered with his ten sons to bid them farewell and commissioned the prime minister of the realm to be their guardian.

Soon after the king had left, the prime minister called all ten of the sons before him to announce the plan of action they would follow while their father was away. Beginning with the oldest, he passed in review over each of the ten brothers. When he finished, he returned to the fourth son. *He is not regal and handsome enough,* the prime minister thought to himself.

After a moment's hesitation, the prime minister ordered the guards to remove the fourth son, banning him from the company of his brothers. Judging his own son to be a finer specimen of royalty and distinction, he inserted him as the fourth of the ten.

In time, the king returned to the palace from his journey and immediately called for his ten sons. One by one he warmly hugged them until he came to the fourth. "This is not my son!" he exclaimed with a look of perplexity. "This is an impostor! What has happened to my son, Prime Minister? Explain if you will!"

"Your majesty, your fourth son did not look like a royal son to me, so I replaced him with my own." The king listened in astonishment. How would the prime minister dare to do such a foolish thing?

"Captain of the guard, return my fourth son to this room immediately!" commanded the king. The officer quickly carried out his order and restored the fourth son to the other nine.

Then the king summarily banned the prime minister from his court, dismissing him from the realm.

In this parable, the king is the Creator God; the ten sons are His Ten Commandments. The prime minister is the church that has supplanted the fourth commandment with a commandment of her own. The King is coming back soon, and He will ask His church what she has done with His fourth commandment.[35]

After this I heard a loud voice of a great multitude in heaven, saying, "Alleluia! Salvation and glory and honor and power to the LORD our God! For true and righteous are His judgments, because He has judged the great harlot who corrupted the earth with her fornication; and He has avenged on her the blood of His servants shed by her."

And I heard, as it were, the voice of a great multitude, as the sound of many waters and as the sound of mighty thunderings, saying, "Alleluia! For the LORD God Omnipotent reigns!" (Revelation 19:1, 2, 6)

END NOTES FOR
Sacred Time unRemembered

1. Jiri Moskala, "The Sabbath in the First Creation Account," *Perspective Digest,* vol. 12, no. 2 (Spring 2007), p. 48. At the time of this writing, Moskala was professor of Old Testament at the Andrews University Theological Seminary, Berrien Springs, Michigan.

2. Des Cummings, Jr., *Original Love* (Fallbrook, California: Hart Books, 2001), p. 112.

3. Norman Gulley, *Satan's Trojan Horse—God's End-Time Victory* (Hagerstown, Maryland: Review & Herald Publishing Association, 2004), pp. 39, 195.

4. Nahum M. Sarna, *Exodus, The JPS Commentary* (Philadelphia: The Jewish Publication Society, 1991), p. 201. Sarna is Professor Emeritus of Biblical Studies at Brandeis University. This statement is quoted by Sigve K. Tonstad, *The Lost Meaning of the Seventh Day* (Berrien Springs, Michigan: Andrews University Press, 2009), p. 115.

5. Moskala, "The Sabbath in the First Creation Account," p. 53.

6. Aleta Bainbridge, "The Cosmic Conflict," *Adventist World,* May 2013, p. 23.

7. Dr. James Dobson, from the introduction promo for the radio talk show *My Family Talk*, spring of 2010. This was a statement of general application not related to the subject at hand.

8. Clinton Wahlen, "What's to Believe About the Bible?" *Adventist Review*, August 25, 2011, p. 24.

9. A statement with reference to the authority of Scripture, used by Dr. R. C. Sproul on his daily radio program *Renewing Your Mind*.

10. John Stott and David L. Edwards, *Essentials: A Liberal-Evangelical Dialogue* (London: Hodder & Stoughton, 1988) pp. 319–320.

11. Edwin de Kock, *Christ and Antichrist in Prophecy and History* (Edinburg, Texas: Diadone Enterprise, 2001), p. 143.

12. Peter Heylyn, *The Historical and Miscellaneous Tracts of the Reverend and Learned Peter Heylyn* (London: Charles Harper, 1681), p. 416, cited in Benjamin G. Wilkinson, *Truth Triumphant* (Pacific Press, 1944), p. 75.

13. Leslie Harding, *The Celtic Church in Britain* (Brushton, New York: Teach Services, Inc., 1995), pp. 78, 79.

14. Summary of Saturday bans as listed by Samuele Bacchiocchi, *From Sabbath to Sunday* (Rome: The Pontifical Gregorian University Press, 1977), p. 197.

15. Quoted in J. H. Merle d'Aubigné, *History of the Reformation of the Sixteenth Century* (Edinburgh: Oliver and Boyd, 1853), bk. 9, chap. 11.

16. Quoted from "The Life of Moses," Lesson 1, Series III (San Antonio, Texas; Bible Study Fellowship International, 1993, 2001), p. 1.

17. Other contemporary Christian apologists who make unsubstantiated claims similar to D. James Kennedy's are: Hank Hanegraaff, *The Bible Answer Book* (Nashville, Tennessee: J. Countryman, 2004), p. 70; Pat Robertson, *The Ten Offenses* (Nashville, Tennessee: Integrity Publishers, 2004), p. 104; and Alex McFarland, *The Ten Most Common Objections to Christianity* (Ventura, California: Regal Books, 2007), p. 136.

18. Historical data about the persecuted church through the medieval centuries with sources are recorded in Benjamin G. Wilkinson, *Truth Triumphant* (Nampa, Idaho: Pacific Press, 1944).

19. Viewing Sunday as a strategy of replacing Christ with an appearance of Christ is from Dr. Norman R. Gulley's article "The Battle Against the Sabbath and Its End-time Importance," *Journal of the Adventist Theological Society,* vol. 5, no. 2 (Autumn 1994), p. 87.

20. Tonstad, *The Lost Meaning of the Seventh Day*, p. 2.

21. Tonstad, *The Lost Meaning of the Seventh Day*, p. 5.

22. Martin Luther, *Auslegung des Alten Testaments* [Commentary on the Old Testament], in *Sämmtliche Schriften* [Collected Writings] (1880), edited by Johann Georg Walch, vol. 3, col. 950. German, translated in *Bible Readings for the Home* (Washington, DC: Review & Herald Publishing Assoc., 1915, 1935, 1942, 1949), p. 375; cited in *The International Standard Bible Encyclopedia*, vol. 4, p. 2632, as *Luther's Works*, vol. 35, p. 330.

23. Tonstad, *The Lost Meaning of the Seventh Day,* p. 497.

24. Tonstad, *The Lost Meaning of the Seventh Day,* p. 123.

25. C. A. Keller, *Das Wort OTH als Offenbarungszeichen Gottes* (Basel: Buchdruckerei E. Haenen, 1946) p. 141, quoted in Tonstad, *The Lost Meaning of the Seventh Day,* p. 123.

26. Pinchas Peli, *The Jewish Sabbath: A Renewed Encounter* (New York: Schocken Books), 1988, p. 90. Quoted in Tonstad, *The Lost Meaning of the Seventh Day,* p. 123.

27. Opening statement, "Are the Sabbath laws binding on Christians today?" by Dr. John McArthur, president of the Master's Seminary near Panorama City, California, and speaker on the daily radio broadcast *Grace to You.* This statement is available at: www.gty.org/resources/questions/QA135

28. Moskala, "The Sabbath in the First Creation Account," p. 46.

29. Nahum M. Sarna, *Genesis,* The IPS Torah Commentary (Philadelphia: Jewish Publication Society, 1989), p. 15.

30. Nicola Nigretti, *Il Septimo Giorno* (Rome: Pontifical Biblical Institute Press, 1973), p. 152.

31. Gerhard S. Hasel, "The Sabbath in the Pentateuch," *The Sabbath in Scripture and History,* Kenneth A. Strand, ed. (Washington, DC: Review and Herald Publishing Association, 1982), p. 23.

32. Moskala, "The Sabbath in First Creation Account," p. 48.

33. Dr. James Dobson, Speech at the Spring Counsel for National Policy, Phoenix, Arizona, February 1998.

34. Illustration is adapted from M. Leslie Rice, *Prove All Things* (Washington, DC: Review & Herald Publishing Association, 1961), pp. 39, 40.

35. This parable appeared in Jeffery O. Brown, "Football or Faith," in the *Adventist Review*, world edition, June 2009, p. 37. It was credited to have come from *A Guide to Parenting: On the Winning Team with Your Children* (Grantham: Stanborough Press, 2003), pp. 169–171. The parable was expanded and edited by Daniel Knauft.

Supporting Exhibits

EXHIBIT #1.

Evangelical leaders urge Saturday Sabbath observance.

A New York minister says that if Jews and Christians would observe Saturday as the Sabbath, it would promote religious unity to a degree never before seen in the history of our civilization.

In a Sunday sermon at the Marble Collegiate Church in New York City, Dr. Ernest R. Palen, of the Reformed Church in America, proposed that Protestants and Catholics alike join Jews in observing the seventh day of the week as a day of worship. "It should not be too great a break for Protestants and Catholics to observe the same Sabbath day that Jesus Himself observed," he said.

A National Council of Churches spokesman said that the loss of Sunday as a day of worship might be healthy for all concerned. He noted that Sunday was picked rather arbitrarily for a day of Christian worship, though some Christian churches, such as the Seventh-day Adventist Church, continue to observe the Bible Sabbath (*The Lake Union Herald*, Berrien Springs, Michigan, April 19, 1966).

Dr. Palen proposed that Pope Paul VI take the initiative. He predicted that if the pontiff designated "the seventh day—the historical and biblical Sabbath—as a day to keep holy," most of the major Protestant bodies "would go along."

"It should not be too great a break for us to observe the same Sabbath Day that Jesus himself observed.

"Our madly rushing, neurotic society needs the therapy of the silence and quietness that flows from a day kept holy, really holy. A day when our thoughts are of God, our actions are tempered by a desire to serve God and our families, a day that is so different from other days that it could make us different in our relationships to God and to our fellow men" (quoted by George Dugan, "Christians Urged to Join Jews in Observing Saturday Sabbath," *New York Times*, March 14, 1966, p. 20).

Dr. Harold Lindsell issued a similar proposal in 1976:

We propose that Saturday be set aside as the day of rest for all people. . . . For Protestants and Catholics it should prove no theological hardship: apart from the fact that our LORD rose from the dead on the first day of the week, there is nothing in Scripture that requires us to keep Sunday rather than Saturday as a holy day. (*Christianity Today*, November 5, 1976, p. 42)

EXHIBIT #2.

An unusual admission from a Christian leader

In November 1893 a convention of four thousand Baptist ministers was held in New York City. An invited guest pastor, Fredrick C. Gilbert was among them on November 13 when noted theologian and author of The Baptist Manual Dr. Edward T. Hiscox spoke. The first ever World's Fair in Chicago had just closed in October, and Dr. Hiscox would now speak to the pastors about the Sunday closing that spanned the six-month fair. Immediately following the speech, Pastor Gilbert spoke with Dr. Hiscox requesting that he might have a copy of the notes of his presentation. From his own hand Dr. Hiscox gave him his original, typewritten discourse with corrections in his own handwriting. Here is a portion of what Dr. Hiscox said:

There was and is a command to "keep holy the Sabbath day," but that day was not Sunday. It will however be readily said, with some show of triumph, that the Sabbath was transferred from the Seventh to the First day of the week, with all its duties, privileges, and sanctions.

Earnestly desiring information on this subject, which I have studied for many years, I ask, where can the record of such a transaction be found? Not in the New Testament, absolutely not. There is no scriptural evidence of the change of the Sabbath institution from the Seventh to the First day of the week.

Of course, I quite well know that Sunday did come into use in early Christian history as a religious day, as we learn from the Christian Fathers and other sources. But what a pity that it comes branded with the mark of Paganism, and Christened with the name of the Sun-God then adopted and sanctified by the Papal apostasy, and bequeathed as a sacred legacy to Protestantism.

Dr. Hiscox's presentation does seem to have raised some eyebrows among attendees at the convention, for, in the January 4, 1894 issue of the widely read Baptist publication *The Examiner*, the following comment appeared, apparently referring to Hiscox's remarks:

Some Baptists are fond of demanding a "Thus saith the Lord" for everything, and profess to accept nothing for which explicit authority cannot be produced from the word of God. Probably not a reader of this paragraph would be willing to follow this principle to its legitimate conclusion. It would involve the immediate return to Sabbath worship.

The source for this exhibit is pastor and editor Donald E. Mansell, who provided the notes of Dr. Hiscox that were given by him to Fredrick C. Gilbert.

EXHIBIT #3.

Historical factors that gave birth to the Sunday Lord's Day.

. . . In the earliest years of Christianity, unlike today, the difference between Christians and Jews wasn't so clear. Christianity had just originated in the land of the Jews. It used only the Jewish Bible. Many of its first and most fervent adherents were Jews. All the original disciples were. Christians worshiped Jesus—a Jew. And in the beginning, many of its holy days such as the Sabbath and Passover (Easter), were celebrated the same time as the Jewish festivals. . . .

This link to the Jews would soon have unfortunate consequences for the Christians. After the death of Nero, who had been favorable to Judaism, the Jews "soon afterward became unpopular in the empire primarily because of their resurgent nationalistic feelings which exploded into violent uprisings almost everywhere."*

After each rebellion, the Romans enacted more anti-Jewish legislation, culminating under Hadrian, who outlawed—often on the pain of death—the practices of Judaism, including circumcision, Torah study, and Sabbath-keeping.

Christians obviously didn't wish to be associated with Jews and, as the anti-Jewish sentiment spread, they tried to separate themselves as much as possible from them, especially as the church became more Gentile and less Jewish.

Historian Samuele Bacchiocchi—who received a PhD, in the 1970s for his dissertation on the change of the Sabbath—wrote that "many Christians did take steps to appear, especially in the imperial city, different and clearly distinct from the Jews in the eyes of the Romans. Under the emperor Hadrian (A.D. 117–118) particularly, a clear differentiation from the Jews became a more urgent necessity, due to the punitive measures taken by the emperor against them." And, according to Bacchiocchi, among the changes the Christians made was to move away from keeping the Fourth Commandment.

"Hadrian's measures," says Bacchiocchi, "particularly hash in Rome, apparently encouraged the predominately Gentile membership in the Church in Rome to emphasize their distinction from Judaism by changing the date and manner of observance of characteristic Jewish feasts, especially the Sabbath, which was changed to Sunday."

Sunday, in many respects, was the logical substitute for Sabbath. Sun cults had become so dominant in the Roman empire that eventually Sunday superceded the primacy of Saturday at just about the same time Christians started preferring Sunday over the Sabbath. Some church fathers devised a theology of Sunday, the first day of the week, as the day when light was first created. Church Fathers

---

* Quoted from Samuele Bacchiocchi, *From Sabbath to Sunday*, Pontifical Gregorian University Press, Rome, 1977, pp. 169, 170.

such as Justin and Jerome were among those who used the creation of light—a symbol of the "Sun of Righteousness"—as the justification for keeping Sunday, not Saturday. Only years later, as sun worship faded in the empire, did Jesus' resurrection on the first day of the week become the primarily accepted reason for Sunday-keeping—one that has persisted to this day.

. . . Of course, the change to Sunday didn't occur overnight. By the time that the Roman Catholic Church assumed not only religious, but political power (about the fifth century A.D.), Sunday had become firmly rooted in Christianity. The Catholic Church, under which Sunday became institutionalized, has claimed credit for the transfer. One Catholic journal—*The Catholic Mirror*—expressed it clearly years ago: "The Catholic Church for over one thousand years before the existence of a Protestant, by virtue of her divine mission, changed the day from Saturday to Sunday."

This explanation was excerpted from The Conflict of the Ages series of pamphlets written by Clifford Goldstein and used by permission.

EXHIBIT #4.

Melanchthon's View of the Sabbath

Despite Luther's integral use of the Ten Commandments in his Large and Small Catechisms and despite Melanchthon's affirmation in the Augsburg Confession that the Ten Commandments have not been abrogated, Melanchthon claimed in that same Confession: "Scripture has abrogated the Sabbath-day; for it teaches that, since the Gospel has been revealed, all the ceremonies of Moses can be omitted." The "Scripture" he offered in substantiation of this claim is an ambiguous reference to Colossians 2:16–23 and an unnamed reference in Romans (probably Romans 14). For the sake of expediency that church order might be maintained, Melanchthon upheld Sunday assembly (Hagstotz and Hagstotz, *Heroes of the Reformation*, p. 171), offering only a supposition in its support: "And yet, because it was necessary to appoint a certain day, that the people might know when they ought to come together, *it appears that* the Church designated the LORD's Day for this purpose; and this day *seems to have been* chosen all the more for this additional reason, that men might have an example of Christian liberty, and might know that the keeping neither of the Sabbath nor of any other day is necessary" (Augsburg Confession, emphasis supplied). Melanchthon's citing of Colossians was in countering Roman Catholic traditions. Thus, in his rationalization of the divinely ordained seventh-day Sabbath, Melanchthon unwittingly called attention to the very reason that Sunday as the day for Christian assembly should be rejected—its authority rests outside of Scripture as a "tradition of men" (Colossians 2:8).

EXHIBIT #5.

Sabbath observance in the Syriac translation of Hebrews 4:9, 10

Evidence from the Syriac version of Hebrews 4:9, 10 attests to the Eastern Church's upholding of Sabbath observance for the believer. G. D. Bauscher's careful translation of the Syriac of the passage reads:

So then it remains for the people of God to keep the Sabbath. Whoever enters His rest, he also has rested from his works as God did from His own.

This passage builds an understanding of the "rest" (*katapausis*) of faith upon an understanding the Sabbath (verse 4) and Sabbath keeping (verses 9, 10). Those who do not understand true Sabbath observance will not understand the value of the comparison. Some seem to think that resting on the Sabbath is an effort to gain God's favor, when it is evidence of the believer's trust in God's provision for their lives (see Exodus 16).

The Sabbath. Notice the specific mention of the Sabbath in the Syriac of verse 4: "According to what He said about *the Sabbath*, 'God rested on the day seventh from *His works* all of them' " (Bauscher, emphasis supplied). It says that God rested from "His works." The phrase reappears in verse 10. Verse 10 says, "Whoever enters His rest, he also has rested from *his works* as God did from His own" (Bauscher, emphasis supplied). The statement parallels the Sabbath commandment (Exodus 20:8–11) and God's explanation of the Sabbath as the sign of the Creation (Exodus 31:15, 17).

Sabbath keeping. In verse 9, the Syriac uses the verb *lamshebatu*, "to keep the Sabbath." The Greek uses *sabbatismos* ("Sabbath keeping") for the "rest" of Hebrews 4:9 and *katapausis* for "rest" everywhere else (Hebrews 3:11, 18; 4:1, 3, 5, 8, 10, 11). Many early authorities attest that *sabbatismos* literally means "Sabbath observance" (see Plutarch, "*De Superstitione*," 3, in *Moralia*, 166a; Justin Martyr, "Dialogues with Trypho," 23.3; Epiphanius, *Panarion*, sect 30, chap. 2, verse 2; *Martyrdom of Peter and Paul*, chap. 1; and *Apostolic Constitutions* 2.36.2).

If *sabbatismos* is taken in a spiritualized manner, verse 10 is contradicted, for no Christian can honestly declare that he has ceased from all his works. Those who say that they have ceased from their works *as a means of salvation* corrupt the parallel of the ceasing of God's works, for God did not cease from bad or unproductive works on the seventh day. The verse only makes complete sense if we understand it to mean that believers cease from labor on the Sabbath as God ceased from His.

The early Christian church found it safe to follow the pattern that Jesus lived as well as the example of the disciples, who knew Jesus' heart most intimately. If is for this "faith once delivered" that Jude urges believers in every succeeding age to contend (Jude 3).

The research for the last two exhibits was provided by Kevin L. Morgan.

Acknowledgements

To Kevin Morgan, M. A., pastor, author, editor and co-author of several historical documentary books defending Christian issues in prophetic inspiration and biblical exegesis. His book *Sabbath Rest*, first drew my attention to his ability to deal accurately with historical documentation. As the current book was written, he discovered several sources of supportive documentation that are in print here for the first time. His editorial skills and attention to detail—added to his deep interest in the subject—has enhanced the easy-flowing, dynamic style of *Sacred Time unRemembered*. His advice, editorial suggestions and dedication were vital in bringing the manuscript to maturity.

Kevin Morgan

To Tim Larson, artist, who gave the book its title: *Sacred Time unRemembered*. He is also the designer of the cover for the book. Tim and Georgina Larson served as volunteer advisers from the inception of the book to its publication in 2014. Georgina's great, great, great great grandfather—a Sabbath-observing Christian—because of persecution, fled his home in Wales to come to America.

To Tony Vargas, web designer of Surge in America.com where *Sacred Time unRemembered* is shown via the Internet.

To Emil H. Knauft, and Marguerite V. Knauft, my parents, who envisioned a rich Christian education for me. Their generous investment made the initial preparation of the current book manuscript possible. Writing the book is a tribute of gratitude to my dear father and mother whose marriage spanned over 72 years until my father's death in 2012.

Marguerite and Emil Knauft

To the friends and volunteers who read the *Sacred Time unRemembered* manuscript (from its early to later stages) giving feedback and encouragement:

Bill Street, Samuel J. Knauft, Darrel Brown, Lyle Albrecht, Kathy Bartlett, Hal Thomsen, Isabelle Session, Jeff Schultz, Claire Beaumont, Zack Hokett, Barry Bussey, Jonathan Ray, Pat Arrabito, Skip McClannahan, Gary Schneider, Delene Janke, Freda Iverson, Steve Leddy, Katelynn Curry, Naira Mirzoyera, Jerry C. Thomas, Greg Bartlett, Tim Larson, Phyllis MacFarland, Kevin Morgan, John Layer, Sandra Pinkoski, Jac Colon, Josh Neff, Bruce Pearson, Marguerite Knauft, Jesse Ferguson, Rebekah Alpisa, Gordon Boggs, Thomas Knauft, Vern Culver, Juanita Boldt, Jesse Session, Alex Arquitt, Georgina Larson, Russel Jurgensen, Diana Bidna, Russell Dunne, Wendy Marcum, Tony Vargas, Vernita Clarembeau Kontz, Dan Moore, Carrie Ferguson, Leon Cornforth, Theodore Knauft, Katherine M. Neff, Barny Shortridge, Suzanne Hafar, Dave Cantrell, Matthew Gilkey, Wayne Harley M.D., Jesse McQuarter, Ron Day, Joan Baker, Nolan Evans, Marci Knauft, Leland Zollinger, Keith Parris, John Darrow, Ella Mae Cuffy, Deborah Hanes, Emil H. Knauft, Donn Leiske, Ken Wilbur, Casey Wolverton, Steve Wall, Munro Maguire, Marius Antalute, Kitty Woodruff.

To the several God-fearing public evangelists who, through the years, have inspired me to urgency in extending the gospel invitation: Robert L Boothby, Dan Caslow, Emil H. Knauft, J. Reynolds Hoffman, Lyle D. Albrecht, Jac Colon, Dave Cantrell, Leon Cornforth, and Steve Wohlberg,

To Johanne Schriever Knauft, my grandmother, a German Lutheran immigrant to America. The untimely death of her nine-year-old son, Willie, led her on a determined search to know the truth about death and the afterlife. At the public gospel presentations of evangelist Charles T. Everson, the evidence of Scripture regarding the resurrection brought solace to her mind and heart. There, as well, she embraced the Creation Sabbath. From them the light of gospel truth was passed on to my family.

To the hand of Providence which I often sensed during the preparation of the manuscript.

Johanne Schriever
Knauft

Charles T. Everson

165

Questions and Answers

Question: I've heard people use Colossians 2:16, 17 to prove there's no longer anything special about the seventh-day Sabbath. A friend who has a Greek study Bible pointed out that the word translated "sabbath" in these verses is the same word used in the Bible for the seventh-day sabbath, not the word used for the Jewish ceremonial feast days.

Answer: I'll begin by quoting the verses in question: "Therefore do not let anyone judge you by what you eat or drink, or with regard to a religious festival, a New Moon celebration or a sabbath day. These are a shadow of the things that were to come; the reality, however, is found in Christ."

The Greek word translated "sabbath" in Colossians 2:16 is sabbaton. This is the same word, whether singular or plural, that's used for "sabbath" everywhere else in the Greek Old and New Testaments.[1] Nothing in the word itself indicates whether it refers to the weekly Sabbath or ceremonial sabbaths.

Some commentators have argued that because sabbaton in Colossians 2:16 is plural, it refers to the weekly Sabbath. Perhaps this is what your friend had in mind. However, the plural of sabbaton is used elsewhere in the New Testament for a single weekly Sabbath.[2] Whether sabbaton refers to weekly or ceremonial sabbaths cannot be decided on the basis of the Greek form of the word. It has to be determined by the context. So let's examine the context.

First, notice that Paul began by admonishing the Colossian Christians to avoid judging each other about certain issues. While I don't believe Paul had in mind the weekly sabbath (the reasons for which I will explain momentarily), his advice applies nicely to the present controversy over whether Sabbath should be celebrated on the first or the seventh day of the week. This doesn't mean we can't have convictions about the day we keep. It means we should avoid questioning the Christian experience of those who differ with us.

Paul mentioned two points in Colossians 2:16 that can help us decide whether the sabbath(s) he referred to was the weekly Sabbath or the yearly ceremonial sabbaths of the Hebrew tabernacle ritual. The first is that "sabbath"

166

was the last of several issues the Colossian Christian apparently were judging each other about. The others were choices of what to eat and drink, religious festivals, and new moon celebrations.

Second, Paul said all of these "are a shadow of the things that were to come; the reality, however, is found in Christ." So Paul wasn't just talking about what people ate and drank at their regular meal time. He had in mind eating and drinking that foreshadowed Christ. He also had in mind the observance of religious festivals and new moon celebrations that pointed forward to Christ.

We know, of course, that the ceremonial law required the Jews to bring a variety of food and drink offerings to the temple as a part of their worship.[3] It also mandated the observance of various holy days through-out the year,[4] and the new moon was to be celebrated on the first day of each month.[5]

All of these were indeed "a shadow of the things that were to come," that is, of Christ's life, death, and resurrection. That's why Paul said "the reality . . . is found in Christ." When Christ came, He fulfilled all these shadows or types, including animal sacrifices, and they ceased to exist. This is consistent with the statement in Hebrews that the entire sanctuary ritual was "a copy and shadow of what is in heaven."[6]

The weekly Sabbath has never been a shadow of anything. The fourth commandment presents the weekly Sabbath as a memorial of Creation: "In six days the Lord made the heavens and the earth, the sea, and all that is in them, but he rested on the seventh day. Therefore [or "that's why"] the Lord blessed the sabbath day and made it holy."

Even at the time the Ten Commandments were given, Creation was an event in the distant past and not a shadow of Christ, whose coming was still future. This rules out the sabbath in Colossians 2:16 being the weekly Sabbath.

On the other hand, all of the ceremonial sabbaths pointed forward to Christ, just as Paul said. Thus, in Colossians 2:16 Paul was referring to the yearly ceremonial sabbaths of the Hebrew tabernacle service, not the weekly Sabbath of the fourth commandment.

Answer is written by Marvin Moore, editor: Signs of the Times Magazine.

Footnotes:
1. The Old Testament was originally written in Hebrew and Aramaic but was translated into Greek a couple centuries before Christ.
2. See, e.g., Matthew 28:1.
3. See, e.g., Leviticus 7:12–18 (food offerings) and 23:13 and Numbers 15:10 (drink offerings).
4. Leviticus 23:4–44
5. Numbers 10:10; 28:11
6. Hebrews 8:5, emphasis supplied.

Question: Doesn't Paul's instruction in Romans 14:5, 6 free the Christian to select his own time of sabbath during the week? The question of a holy day is one of personal preference, isn't it?

Answer: I'll begin by quoting these two verses from the New King James Version: "One person esteems one day above another; another esteems every day alike. Let each be fully convinced in his own mind. He who observes the day, observes it to the Lord; and he who does not observe the day, to the Lord he does not observe it."[1.]

Christians who keep Sunday as the Sabbath sometimes use these verses as evidence that any day is OK to keep. "Saturday is fine," they say, "but so is Sunday or Wednesday or any other day of the week that one chooses. What's important is to keep one day out of seven." According to this argument, the requirement of the fourth commandment to observe only the seventh day of the week is no longer binding upon Christians.

We believe the fourth commandment still requires observance of the Saturday Sabbath—the seventh day. [2.] So how do we respond to Paul's statement in Romans 14:5, 6?

The first thing to notice is that the word Sabbath does not appear in these verses, nor do the words "seventh day" or "first day." So the question is whether Paul was discussing whether the fourth commandment should be observed on the seventh day or the first day of the week when he wrote these words. It's easy for us, living in the twenty-first century, to assume that he was, since there's quite a debate in our culture over whether the Saturday or Sunday is the proper day to keep. But did such a controversy exist in the New Testament church?

The answer is, No, and this text does not prove that there was.

I'm sure there are those who will disagree with my statement that there is no New Testament evidence of a debate over whether the seventh day or the first day of the week is the proper day to keep. The best reason I can give you that indeed there was no such controversy is the New Testament's absolute silence on this issue.

I assume you are sufficiently familiar with the New Testament epistles to know that there was a huge controversy in the New Testament church over circumcision. Conservative Jews insisted that in order to become Christians, Gentiles had to become Jews first, primarily through submission to the rite of circumcision. Paul said No, this was not necessary, and he opposed these Jews throughout his ministry. Galatians 5:1-15 is probably his strongest response to this question.[3.]

Had Paul or any other apostle advocated a change of the Sabbath from the seventh to the first day of the week, I can assure you that conservative Christian Jews would have been absolutely outraged and at least as vocal in their opposition as they were to Paul's insistence that Gentiles need not be circumcised.

But there isn't a shred of evidence that conservative New Testament Jews were upset over a chance of the Sabbath from the seventh to the first day of the week. Thus it seems rather obvious that there was no such controversy. And if there was no Sabbath-Sunday controversy back then, then that isn't the issue Paul was discussing in Romans 14:5, 6. To say that it was is to read our debates back into his time.

So what did he have in mind? The most frequently mentioned possibility is the Old testament ceremonial feast days, such as Passover, Pentecost, and the Day of Atonement. There is some evidence of contention over this issue in the New Testament church,[4] so it is reasonable to read this into Paul's words in Romans 14:5, 6. However, Paul himself didn't say that's what he meant.

Having said all of this, I will conclude with what I believe is a reasonable application of Paul's words to our issues, even if he wasn't directly addressing them. Basically, Paul was advising Christians to respect each others convictions, even though they might disagree with them. While it's perfectly appropriate to hold strong convictions over the right day to celebrate the Sabbath (Paul did say that "each one should be fully convinced in his own mind,")[5] we must also respect each others choices, even where we disagree with them. We should not judge anyone to be a non-Christian simply because of his or her choice of a day to keep.

Answer is written by Marvin Moore, editor of Signs of the Times Magazine

Footnotes:
1. New King James Version, italics supplied
2. In the strictest sense, Saturday isn't the Sabbath. Saturday begins and ends at midnight, while the Sabbath begins at sundown on Friday and ends at sun down on Saturday (see Leviticus 23:32).
3. See also Romans 2:25-29.
4. See for example Galatians 4:10
5. NIV

Question: I've heard the fourth commandment explained by Bible teachers and friends that one day out of seven is what is meant. Most Christians meet together on the first day—doesn't that meet the specification of the commandment? Isn't it most important that God is being worshiped?

Answer: Truly, that our lives are devoted to God is paramount. Many regard a life that is being lived for Jesus—practicing His presence—is a gift of worship each moment of every day. Do you not agree that the Bible believer who is devoted to God is also seeking to know the expressed will of God for his or her life?

With this in mind, the question regarding the fourth commandment must be answered. In all of the Bible, where can the idea be found that God's holy day is left for mortal humans to decide? All Bible believers agree that the first day of the week is when Jesus triumphantly rose from the grave; they also know that Jesus was crucified on Friday, the sixth day of the week. Jesus rested in the tomb over the Sabbath of the fourth commandment on the seventh day of the week—Saturday. No Jew or Gentile Christian in the first century would think to view as holy time any other day of the week.

A precedent had been established thousands of years before. At Mt. Sinai, the Creator God spoke audibly to the two million freed slaves in the desert—"the seventh day is the Sabbath of the Lord thy God." In the fourth commandment, God Himself states the foundation upon which the seventh day is sacred time—"for in six days the LORD made the heavens and the earth . . . and rested the seventh day . . ."(Exodus 20:10). Only one day of the week was blessed and "set apart" by God—the seventh day—what we call Saturday.

So the question persists—where in Scripture did the Creator alter the foundation of sacred time set at Creation? What mortal human is willing to assume such a divine task and claim that everyone is now free before the Creator God to pick and choose whatever day suits him or her?

Millions of Sabbath-observing Jews since the time of Christ still confirm the Saturday Sabbath. So have unnumbered Christian believers during the medieval centuries confirmed it in martyrdom for their faithfulness to God's holy day.

Who is willing to say that the passing of time over centuries is enough to change what is always truth—God's expressed will in Scripture? Do not Jesus' words still matter: "Render to Caesar the things that are Caesar's, and to God the things that are God's" (Mark 12:17)?

God has identified the Sabbath as "the holy day of the LORD honorable, . . ." (Isaiah 58:13). Jesus Christ's personal practice honored this as well (Luke 4:16).

How to begin
observing the Sabbath

Step 1: Thank Jesus. It is not by happenstance that you are interested in observing the Sabbath of the Lord. God's Word has informed you of His will; the Holy Spirit, the Spirit of truth has brought conviction to you. It is important to act when He is impressing you. Thank Him just now for revealing His will to you. John 16:13.

In your decision to observe the Bible Sabbath, be assured that you are not leaving behind your past experience in Jesus Christ. Rather, you are advancing in added appreciation and understanding of what it means to be in fellowship with Jesus. And you are not leaving behind your family and friends, but you are shining a light on the path ahead for them as well.

Step 2: Tell someone the decision you've made. Announce your decision to a friend or family member, and share what this means to you. Even inviting someone to support you in your decision will strengthen your resolve to initiate this milestone in your life. Being proactive about your decision will give those closest to you the sense of delight and conviction upon which your decision is made. Your example is also a strength of influence for others in your life.

Step 3: You are not alone! Identify other Christian friends who will support your decision. A Sabbath-observing group or church family will be close by. You may wish to choose someone as a coach who will come alongside of you and answer your questions, giving direction for a meaningful Sabbath experience. Mutually shared experiences with others gives the opportunity to see God "close up" through Bible study, personal testimonies, praise singing, and the proclamation of God's Word. Your early experiences with Sabbath observance is a learning curve—give yourself time to grow into this dimension of your walk with Jesus.

Step 4: Give priority to the Sabbath day. Jesus is calling you to spend 24-hours (the seventh day) with Him consistently. This appointment begins at sunset on Friday (Leviticus 23:32; Mark 1:32). Begin to view "sacred time" as the high point of your week. A new Sabbath life-style takes time and planning. God calls it "holy" time. This boundary, set at the Creation, is a distinction between "work" and "rest." Begin to think of your choices for the Sabbath with this distinction. The formula presented by God Himself (Isaiah 58: 13,14) and the example set by Jesus' Sabbath observance will provide the principles for making decisions about Sabbath activities. Your choices will become a model for others.

Step 5: Here's what to expect. 1. Expect all the other salvation truths of the Bible to mean more to you. 2. Expect your interest in the salvation of lost people to increase. 3. Expect to be misunderstood by others for your decision to observe the Sabbath. 4. Expect someone to challenge your decision and describe your actions as legalistic; expect them to say this matter is not important—how could so many people be wrong? Remember, most people do not have the historical reference point upon which to base an intelligent decision. 5. Expect to sincerely be asked why you are beginning to observe the Sabbath—this is your opportunity to extend understanding. 6. Expect the Holy Spirit to guide your mind in answering questions. 7. Expect that when Jesus rescues His people—both resurrected and translated—to take them to the Father's house (John 14:1-3) many will only then experience their first seventh-day Sabbath (Isaiah 66: 22:23). 8. Expect to find contentment that you are responding to the Savior's invitation to joyfully experience the Sabbath fellowship—He welcomes you!

Because you are choosing to begin this journey, the seventh-day Sabbath has been brought out of its exile—out of the "cob-webbed halls of forgetfulness." Through you, it is on display again. You are bringing honor to our Creator. Praise God!

Do you have a message or comment to give the author?
email: deknauft@hotmail.com

Supportive website for:
Sacred Time unRemembered

surgeinamerica.com

Advancing the blessing and delight of the
original Lord's day!

A R T I C L E S

• Resting in Grace
• The Old "Jewish Sabbath"
• The Sabbath in First Creation Account
• How to Honor the Resurrection of Jesus

S T O R I E S   O F
S A B B A T H   P R O V I D E N C E

M O R E
Q U E S T I O N S   &   A N S W E R S

B O O K S T O R E

Torch*light*
INTELLIGENCE.COM

Revealing the road ahead
Isaiah 62:1

St. Johns bridge - Portland, Oregon —photo by © hollyknauft.c